Re-Routed
Verse for the Human Animal

Re-Routed
Verse for the Human Animal

Francesca Marguerite Maximé

Blue-Cream Books
Brooklyn, NY

Blue-Cream Books
Brooklyn, NY 11218

First Edition
Set in Cambria

Layout by Francesca Marguerite Maximé
Cover Font, "Ella," by Alexander Norelli
Cover Design by Alexander Norelli   www.alexnorelliart.com
Author Photo, Emily Klassen Wilson www.emilybphotography.com
Cover Illustration: "The Tree of Life"
© Claudia 'Cotrutza' French   www.cotrutza.com

ISBN-13: 978-0615802084
ISBN-10: 0615802087

www.facebook.com/ReRoutedBook
www.francescamaxime.com
www.facebook.com/FrancescaMaximeTVHostPoet
www.pw.org/content/francesca_marguerite_maxime
www.nyqpoets.net/poet/francescamaxime

Re-Routed

Verse for the Human Animal

Acknowledgements

"My Grandmother Sends Me Silky Nightgowns" - *Lips*
"The Spinster" – *Lips*
"Biting My Nails" – *Lips*
"Pinocchio" – *Paterson Literary Review*

I am entirely grateful to Maria Mazziotti Gillan, Laura Boss, Richard Blanco, Jim Reese, Dorianne Laux, Alexander Norelli, Claudia French, Matt Garrison, Fortuna Sung, Jesse Jones, Romain Collin, Wayne Westerfield, Annika Barriteau-Terrell, and especially, my mother, Dr. Janet Magnani, for their guidance and support.

For my mother, who chose me, and whose love knows no bounds.

Contents

*"If you do not change direction,
you may end up where you are heading."*

Lao Tzu

Re-Routed
Verse for the Human Animal

ONE: Re-Routed

STILLBORN

If you had a baby and it was born dead
would you still have a celebration, or a funeral

Would you ask someone to be the one
to cut the cake or open the gifts
while you pumped the unused milk from your breasts

Or would you instead
prepare the tiny body for burial
and place sheets over mirrors, to mourn

DRIVE

In my grey Volvo chariot
that used to be my mother's
I drive too fast to my new job in New Jersey
and twice get pulled over
for going thirty miles an hour over the speed limit

Perhaps that's always been my problem:
trying to get somewhere too fast
and missing the beauty that's revealed
in slowing down along the way

Like trying to get my ex-fiancé to marry me
after three years together, because it was time
then accepting his proposal a year after we'd broken up
because he'd finally felt the pressure of the ultimatum
And then dealing with the crash
of what it meant to my life
when two days before the wedding
he said he didn't know himself and wouldn't marry me

Material in my first book was written over eight years
and spanned my childhood to my breakup and beyond
It contained stories about the damage
that came from my own lack of marriage
and the new difficulty I had with weddings
The poems I'd written were called lies
some couldn't bear to see
and caused my first book to become
a limited edition seen or read by few

I vowed that day to keep writing
to keep singing without the crow on my shoulder:
to knock off that bird, that crackly voice
and replace it with a new song

I vowed to stay in the right hand lane
use my radar detector
and take my time getting to where I need to be

This detour was unexpected
but I'm more comfortable in my seat
I feel good about where I'm headed

My compass is set North
I'll keep on driving
and I'm enjoying the ride

PHYRRHULOXIA

My crow has been replaced by Phyrrhuloxia:
that grey and red cardinal-like bird from the Southwest

I'd never seen one before my mother's friend in Phoenix
posted photos of the bird in her backyard, online

Phyrrhuloxia has ousted
the black crow of fear from its perch,
since the red Northeast cardinal no longer protects me:
my grandfather's favorite bird

Instead, that grey and red songbird
has become my new voice
She created my first book-child:
one that while stillborn, is vibrant even in death

I'd written about the breakup with my ex
my mother, father and family
I'd written about my issues of self-doubt:
my concerns with weight and appearance while on TV

That new voice, once she began singing, was silenced
Not everyone liked Phyrrhuloxia's refrain
Still, I embrace this gentle and fiery red and grey bird
found in the desert, along with bighorn sheep and prairie dogs

I hear her chirping, no matter the distance between us
chanting sweet melodies that need to be sung

TWO: Animals

LIONS

As I watch the 60 Minutes tape
of the two documentarians
show mighty Tao, the amazing lioness,
lose one of her three cubs to a crocodile
and the other to a stampede of water buffalo
I see her come back to one baby lion
She tries to kick it, grab it, drag it, and hold it
hoping its back isn't truly broken,
wanting it to run freely as it did just moments before
Instead, with its supple spine flattened, this little lion cub
drags its body forward on two paws towards its mother
She returns to look at him
Golden fur: short, plush, sturdy
She puts the lion cub down,
stares outward into the willowy plains
blinks hard, and holds her stare forward
She does not look back, and marches on

I am reminded of the day I took my Baby Lion
on a plane trip to Florida
to interview for my new job in Pensacola
I thought I had taken him off the plane with me
but instead he was wrapped up in the plane blanket,
having served as my pillow
Even after seven years of service, I needed him
I didn't know who to call or what to say
A lost stuffed animal is not a lost child or lost pet
or even a lost piece of luggage

But Baby Lion meant so much more to me
than my favorite black shirt or pair of jeans
So much more than my watch, books or hair dryer
So much more than any of my papers

Baby Lion was my heart
He had steered me through the years of emotional turmoil
that followed my breakup with my ex-fiancé
During the years my ex and I were together
Baby Lion was there for fun and to be my pal:
a companion when my love and I weren't together

I watch this lion-baby on screen,
left alone in the tall grass, with a broken back
I think of my Baby Lion,
left alone on a plane going who-knows-where

I see that lioness face away from her cub,
now left to die. She marches forward

The documentarians say: *You can see the pain in her face*
Her eyes blink, hard. Her mouth opens in a silent howl

They say her survival instincts have taken over
She knew when to leave. She knew she had to move on

HORSES

Seeing the video of the horse whisperer train
this unusually yellow, golden horse
I'm reminded of how beautiful, strong and perfect
these creatures are: how they were made to carry us
and roam wild and free

They tell the story of how this three-year-old horse
was born with oxygen depletion
How its mother was unable to care for it after birth
How it may have suffered brain damage
How it essentially became an orphan

In the documentary on horse training
the horse whisperer is asked to help this horse
The film explains how the trainer and his brother
were physically beaten by their father growing up
The trainer, from age three until high school,
in attacks that got worse when his mother died
and only stopped when his football coach
noticed welts on his back in the locker room
The horse trainer talks to the horse's owner
The woman says her golden boy's an uncastrated
stallion kept for breeding. That he roams free
at her ranch, with eighteen other horses just like him

She says he's always been a problem
She explains when she once tried
to separate him from approaching visitors,
her yellow boy unexpectedly turned,
lunged toward her golf cart,
and broke her back in two places

The trainer tells the woman she'd taken on too much
That those studs were too wild and needed help
That castration would calm them down
He says he could see just how defiant
and unrelenting this horse was: how the stud's pain,
like his own father's rage, knew no bounds

Still, unlike the terror he felt towards his father
the horse whisperer saw the yellow horse
for what he was: a wounded, neglected child
His handler tried to take hold of the half-ton animal
as it tossed its blonde mane,
sneered and kicked up its legs

With the trainer's guidance, the handler
quieted the horse and saddled him
Trotted him around the corral,
delighting amazed onlookers

Until this horse, this golden boy
this three year old stud colt, this blonde bombshell
Suddenly turned on the gentle handler and began
to disobey the soothing sounds of the horse whisperer
Instead of obliging and trusting as he'd
learned to do just moments before,
the horse lurched forward, bit the handler on the forehead
and created a deep gash requiring stitches
The unbridled horse continued to buck and kick up,
unable to escape its own frustration in that pen

The horse's owner shakes her head
Says she has to put him down
That he's not suited for rehabilitation
That he's unsafe to be around

The horse whisperer says the owner may have
brought the horse to him believing it's the problem
but that in fact, it's the owner
who may need to look in the mirror

She cries. The trainer sees the pain in her face
and feels for the golden boy, saying
if the horse would have had a different early life,
then perhaps—even if deprived of oxygen at birth—
with the proper attention, love and training
he too, could have been a kind and gentle horse:
one that both children and adults could safely ride

The horse whisperer says he knows in his heart
this golden boy was only treating others
the way he felt he had been treated
That today, no amount of love
he or the owner could give him
would be enough to save him

The trainer swishes brightly-colored flags
in front of the stud on that sun-soaked Montana ranch
He gets the horse to move from the grassy corral
into the steel highway trailer on its own

Perhaps even this neglected, brain-damaged horse
knew when a golden opportunity had been squandered

Perhaps even this golden boy, this stunning stud
knew when it was time to let it all go

COYOTE

PART I

This wild, female animal
orphaned by its mother,
left in pillows of snowy woods
while her brothers wander their own trails,

seeks sustenance for survival
She approaches the open plain:
her paw prints dot the pure white fluff

Under a large pine, something moves
She inches towards it, hoping for dinner
She's hungry, starving

Snap!
The steel jaw
clamps down hard

No food
Still hungry
Alone

PART II

Gnawing at her own paw,
she tries to escape
A man tracks her prints in the snow
and calls animal rescue

They unbind the trap
They triage this wild coyote
They muzzle her, tranquilize her
and mend her paw

They feed her, water her
They watch her grow stronger
She drinks and eats more
Her coat becomes slick again,
her eyes, clearer

One day they say:
It's time to let her go
She's finally made it

The man turns away for a moment
It is then, she strikes,

clamping down the same way
the steel trap snapped down on her
Her incisors, enjoying the soft flesh
she'd long sought

Tasting the fresh blood
she had become herself fully,
pouncing without hesitation:
Her survival instincts kicked in
She'd bode her time well

Instead of bearing healthy cubs
she instead passes on her disease
to those with whom she's found shelter

Now, there's no longer a place
for sick coyotes to go:
no trackers remain to find them

This female coyote, now satisfied:
free to seek her cravings
Again able to roam without hindrance,
in search of her next kill

MY MOTHER'S BUREAU

My first cat Lily had her first litter
in the bottom drawer of my mother's claw-footed bureau
She chose the underwear drawer because it was soft
and while my mother didn't have much silky underwear
she did have a few silky nightgowns

My mother, a doctor, never had pets growing up
and didn't realize it would have been a good idea
to get an outdoor cat like Lily spayed
I was five when I remember seeing her in that drawer
The mucus and amniotic fluid all in a puddle
with my mother's cotton underwear and a pile of wet kittens

There were five of them, so small
I remember their little pink tongues and tiny teeth
Their miniscule mouths, sucking on Lily's teats
She wasn't an especially friendly cat
and often went out hunting for birds and mice
While she occasionally slept outside overnight,
mostly, she slept with me and kept me warm

There's a photograph of me with those kittens
after they'd grown to be a few weeks old
My long dark hair in ringlets, parted in the middle
held on each side with plastic *bolitas*—pony tail holders

Sitting on the back porch in springtime
with the Angelini girls, Martha and Louise
We held a kitten in each hand,
displaying them for the photo,
proud of these little fur creatures:
amazed by their gaping mouths and growing paws

It was from the same back porch
I used to spin and throw Lily
I'd torture that cat in a way
only someone with evil would

I'd turn around and around, again and again
up on the porch and then throw her off
I'd wait to see if in fact she'd land on two feet
I'd laugh at how, based on the centrifugal force of my whirls,
she'd end up only being able to walk in circles—
not a straight line—for nearly a minute

I don't know if my half-brother spun Lily first
and if that's where I got the idea
But I know I whirled her around and tossed her
at least once, just to show him what it looked like
This cat, this same creature I'd snuggle with at night
This mother toward whom I became the animal

This morning, my kitty Louisa walks towards me
on the parquet floor in a straight line with a visible limp
I don't know why she can't put as much weight
on her front paw as she used to. I do know
part of the reason her leg may be injured is because
I might have thrown her off my high bed too often,
or a bit too roughly, after she'd started licking my face
when it was still dark at five A.M.

The veterinarian said it was a spinal injury and gave her antibiotics
and a cortisone shot But Louisa isn't getting any better. I have pet
insurance and could take her back in for an x-ray, but my mother asks
if I really want to know what they might find:

Arthritis?
There's nothing to be done about it
She's already nine and could be starting to show her age
Cancer?
What kind of treatment does one reasonably give a cat,
even if you have pet insurance
A broken bone?
One that hadn't healed well would serve as a reminder
that perhaps it really was me that caused her pain

Louisa, this cat, has saved my life more than once
She's seen me through my breakup, my first book
my moves to Florida and New York City

With her soft grey fur mottled with orange and cream
she's been a little Buddha resting peacefully on her bed
Sometimes, she even snores when she sleeps
She paws at the refrigerator door for a taste of Greek yogurt

She meows
when I first walk in after work and greets me
She jumps in my bed
only when the lights are out for the night

To think I used to torture my first cat, Lily
and revel in her confusion, disgusts me
To think I may have caused Louisa harm,
disturbs me just as much

I wish I could stuff
all my animal instincts
into the bottom drawer
of my mother's bureau and seal it

But like the meows from Lily's kittens
birthed in a pile of cotton underwear and silky nightgowns
My bad behavior—those animal instincts—
still cries to be let out

ANIMAL RESCUE

I do charity work for an animal rescue cause
in New York City. It's not hands-on
like cleaning litter boxes or calling people
to find homes for cats and dogs
I host events where they serve wine and cheese
and where pet owners can bring their pups
dressed up in fancy costumes
They're often held on the red carpet
with celebrities in attendance
(The organizers say I'm one of them)

I ask my producers at the TV station
to do a segment on the morning news
featuring animals up for adoption
Without the money raised at our cocktail parties
one hundred and forty cats and dogs
are euthanized in New York City each week

I think of my kitty Louisa
who has been at my side nine years and counting
I see her limp and hear her wheeze and think
she's not quite the kitten she was
when I brought her home in Binghamton

I was on my way to church when
I found an ad for kitties in the newspaper:
twenty dollars, a month or two old,
fed and de-wormed

Hoping one would christen our new home,
I skipped church, woke my fiancé
and drove to the shelter
(which was actually just a woman's house)

We sat on the sofa as the black and white kitten
rolled the tinker balls on the floor around us
The woman showed us a slightly older tiger kitten
who looked like the first cat I'd ever owned, Lily

The woman kept asking us
if we wanted to see the Blue-Creams
I asked, *What's a Blue-Cream?*
because I didn't know

She brought down a little grey and orange bundle
the size of one and a half hands
It ran right up to me and my ex, dashed about
and then raced around with the other kitties

She must have thought it was some kind of audition,
or perhaps she was just being herself
She nosed her way up onto our palms
and saddled up next to us. My ex, who's not
an animal person, exclaimed: she chose us

Instead of church, we went to Wal-Mart
I bought food, toys and a bed Louisa still sleeps on
She saw me through the days my ex broke up with me
and the dark times that followed

She came with me to Florida. We lived
in a beautiful, sunny condo with a patio
She was happy when I left the door open
so she could trot out and watch the birds at the feeder

And although she may not have liked
the tiger print and black velvet tulle party dresses
adorned with sequins and rhinestones
I bought for her to wear when I had company,
she tolerated them

She was always in the room,
no matter how many people
A social, people-person kind of cat:
she kind of reminded me of me

As she sits in my Brooklyn studio apartment alone
while I'm away on writing retreat this weekend
I think of how three days is as long as I can go
without snuggling with Louisa: without her
waking me up with sandpaper tongue kisses

They say dogs are man's best friend
Perhaps cats are a woman's?
I think of how many times this fur-baby has saved my life
Animal rescue turned around. Cat saving human

THREE: History

BAGGAGE

Liz Taylor brought sixty-seven pieces
of Louis Vuitton luggage
with her on a trip to Morocco
Sixty-seven pieces is so much baggage
regardless of whether or not it's high-end
or what's stuffed inside

Mine isn't so high-end
It isn't so pretty or fancy
I used to be classier than I am now
Today, I feel like everyone else:
drained and grey

I used to carry Italian designer handbags from Fendi
with handles like Hermès Birkin bags
I donned silk Valentino gowns, satin Versace dresses
Carried a red Ferragamo purse
Wore four-inch Stuart Weitzman pumps

I used to research the restaurants I'd go to on Zagat's
and only go to the ones deemed
trendy or good for people watching
Or, the ones which had a twenty-eight rating
for ambiance and décor
even if the food was only a twenty-three or twenty-four

While my ex had money with the family business
he'd noted we'd both gone to school in Boston
He, Northeastern. I, an Ivy. But I never felt
my degree made me better than he was

I was drawn to his regality:
the length of his neck, the darkness of his eyes
His grandfather had been an architect
to the former President of France

I felt with him, a princess
in a way I never expected to feel
Royal, in so many ways
is how I thought we looked together

I'd already spent a lifetime
behind velvet ropes interviewing
Hugh Jackman, Donna Karan and President Clinton
I'd already spent a lifetime getting into
exclusive clubs, because the doormen
thought I'd look better inside, than in line

What he and I created when we entered a room
I have no name for
It's what made him say to me when making love once
that we'd have beautiful children together

We'd have been siblings, were we not lovers:
our dark features so similar, but distinct
I was told I resembled Sophia Loren and his mother
My ex, a cross between Andy Garcia and Robert De Niro

He had no luggage for our first two-week trip:
a newly-engaged, pre-wedding honeymoon
With my encouragement
he bought a Samsonite set in grey, not black
(because distinct luggage is good
when looking for your bags at the airport)

Living in the same city for so long
he hadn't needed a passport before then, either
We spent the extra money to have one expedited
to New York City before our departure from JFK

We packed up that new luggage, took off
for the Caymans, and sailed into our new life
We went on catamaran rides, swam with stingrays,
and bumped into people we knew from home—
including the girl he broke up with to be with me—
who'd since married a wealthy businessman from town

Our relationship proved as tumultuous
as that of Elizabeth Taylor and Richard Burton
I never got those big diamonds, though
Instead I received a camera for Christmas

We never married, divorced and remarried
like that celebrity couple,
even though in my eyes,
we were always celebrities

He, my Richard Burton until the day I die:
someone I can never fully escape
Someone, like baggage packed with too many clothes
I could never fully contain

IT WASN'T SUPPOSED TO BE THIS WAY

It wasn't supposed to be this way
Me at forty-one,
living in a studio apartment in Brooklyn
instead of down the street
in the Wright-like glass and stone home we renovated
with stainless steel and granite:
a home that sits on ten acres in the dense Vestal brush
A home in which you still live

It wasn't supposed to be this way
Me, without a husband, after you chose not to marry me
two days before our wedding, now nearly eight years ago

It wasn't supposed to be this way
Me, going to the fertility clinic alone
Spending thousands of dollars on tests
to find out if can still get pregnant (I can)
if I ever did want to have a biological child

It wasn't supposed to be this way:
me, going over profiles of sperm donors
who describe themselves in booklets with photos
with captions like:
5'11, looks like Brad Pitt
with a Masters in Economics
(There's a waitlist for his sperm:
he's what's called a "hot donor")

It wasn't supposed to be this way
My first book, shelved, after someone didn't like it
after I'd poured my heart into my project:
I didn't know that in so doing,
I'd "poked the bear," as they say

It wasn't supposed to be this way
Me, searching for love online
Match.com, JDate, eHarmony, IvyDate,
Chemistry.com, OKCupid, HowAboutWe,
and even the Armenian site, HyeSingles
(even though I'm not Armenian, or Jewish)

Men can sniff out that desperation for love
just as easily as a dog sniffs out other animals
and even though I'm not as desperate as I used to be
I'm probably still desperate enough
to have someone be able to pick up that scent

If I could, I'd tell my ex
I'm sorry, I'm so sorry
for all the things I didn't do right
when we were together:
for all the things I didn't know then
that I know now
I wouldn't have shared things about us
you found embarrassing
I wouldn't have told you
to stand up to your stepmother
when all you really wanted
was your father's approval

I wouldn't have drank as much wine
or cooked as much food
or invited as many people
over to our home as often as I did
I would have respected
that you wanted more private time
and that you wanted more of me to yourself

It wasn't supposed to be this way, us apart
Each of us still unmarried at forty-one and forty-two

Last time we spoke
you said you were in a serious relationship
Still, I am the only one
to have ever worn your mother's ring

KEEP LOOKING

I keep looking for you,
even though it won't be you:
a tall, dark and handsome man

6'2 or six foot at least
Dark brown eyes, full eyebrows,
a full head of black or dark brown hair

I search the online ads and put in
the exact criteria you hold
I half-expect you to pop up,
but of course you don't
since I'm searching in New York City,
and besides, you're too private
to ever look for a girlfriend online

Still, when the 6'2 Jewish lawyer emailed me
and said he wanted to get together,
even though he was just thirty-one, I couldn't resist
Because he reminded me of you
and even though he was not you
he was tall and dark like you
and had money and good taste like you

Of course, a man ten years younger than me
who looks like you
but who doesn't want to get married
will never be my next fiancé

But you, my ex, remain
imprinted in my patterns
as I hold the remote control to my life
and keep looking for the right channel

HOW HE SEES ME

Last night, my friend Jim tells me
I'm a beautiful, generous person
He says he wants "the old Fran" back:
the one he knew when I first
moved to Binghamton fifteen years ago
He was a cameraman and I a new reporter
at the local TV station where he still works

We became fast friends
He taught me all I needed to know about
how to write for TV and the industry's jargon:
A VO/SOT: short for "voiceover;"
something the news anchor typically reads
SOT or "sound on tape," a sound bite
A package, a story the reporter voices over

I lived in a four hundred dollar a month
two-bedroom apartment in Vestal
I often invited our producer Lisa
and her husband over for dinner
(I also dated the other cameraman,
but never let anyone else know:
it was my first job after all)

I was coming off having lost thirty-five pounds
in Overeaters Anonymous in Boston
I was twenty-eight, fresh-faced and enthusiastic
I didn't know what I was doing yet
but I was excited about my new career

Last night, staying at my friend Jim's house,
he tells me reading my first book made him sad
He tells me it's not the person he wants to see
and it's not the person he knows I used to be

I wonder if I'll ever get back to that place
of un-brokenness. Of being broken,
but not knowing that you are, so you
go about life with a kind of wide-eyed-ness
I only see anymore in deer and in babies

Last night, we went on a Scavenger Hunt
through downtown Binghamton
We visited city landmarks I hadn't been to in years
We scoured around for required objects, including:
a Manley's Mighty Mart receipt,
our photo taken in front of the red neon
Greyhound Terminal sign,
and a picture of us riding the elevator
at Boscov's department store

Last night, my friends were excited
I was willing to venture out
to this place I once called home:
to this worn-down city I love
and would have stayed in forever,
had my ex not backed out on marrying me

My friend's wife says she feels a difference in me:
that I've shifted and am not quite as sad as I once was
It's taken me eight years to drive down State Street
and not notice my ex's office building on the corner

I hope my friends are right and I can go back fifteen years:
host dinner parties, go on scavenger hunts
and babysit their children without thinking about
the ones I don't—and may never—have

Back at the bar, after we'd finished the race,
while the organizers tallied up points for prizes,
I looked at the men who were standing there:
some tall, dark and handsome like my ex,
and wondered if I'd be a winner that night

I went to the bathroom,
fixed my hair and put on some fresh lipstick:
unsure of what I'd say or do,
if he were the next person
to walk through the front door

IT'S BEEN EIGHT YEARS SINCE MY EX AND I BROKE UP

It is been nearly eight years since my ex and I broke up
Today I'm back in the city where we used to live
Driving here from Brooklyn, where I live now,
I realized even though I cried in the car this morning
when I said to myself
a piece of my heart will always be with him, I realize
I'm not still stuck in the same place I was
when I came here three years ago

Then, I was mourning, fresh and raw:
unable to look at the tall birch, chatty birds
and elegant deer eating under the trees
The simple smell of fresh fall air
made me shudder and shake:
a permanent reminder of the life I used to have

Today, snow covers the ground
My old house still sits a mile away from this classroom
My old friends still live a half a mile down the street
Even the sign for the Superstar car wash—where my ex
used to take his Audi—still shines in loud,
bright orange letters punctuated with a huge yellow star

Somehow, though, driving along Route 17 and Route 7
the Vestal Parkway, I-84, and 380 didn't hurt so much:
I didn't feel I was still attached to something I knew was lost,
like a butcher's hand, stuck in the meat grinder

Instead, I'm coming back, waving a white flag—
not to make peace with my ex as I had when we met here
for the first time since we broke up, three years ago—
but instead, just be here in a way I haven't been able to be
To reclaim some of the same girl I was
when I moved here fifteen years ago, before we'd ever met:
the independent journalist excited about her new job
(It's the reason why I'd gone there in the first place)

The other day, I had a date in a Brooklyn wine bar with a
twenty-nine year-old financial whiz who spoke Aramaic
He'd spent a year in Europe consulting to the Troika on the
Greek financial crisis. He asked why, when he'd requested
I write a poem for him, I said I couldn't do it

I told him most of my poetry was revealing and raw:
that mainly, I wrote about what I knew well,
and since I didn't really know him yet
I couldn't write something authentic
Instead, I sent him one about my grandfather's tomatoes
and how we in the family can't grow them like he used to

I told him how my first book was mainly about my ex
and his breaking up with me two days before our wedding
(which probably wasn't a good idea if I wanted a second date)

I thought about how I used to feel on dates
two years ago when I thought of that breakup:
how then, I fought for words to describe
how it was behind me (when it really wasn't)

Driving to poetry class today my body does not respond
with excitement or sadness to the "Welcome to Binghamton" sign
as it once did. It doesn't quiver, sitting in this classroom:
the same classroom in which I took classes
when my ex and I were together and we lived up the street

Today, my body has moved on
Perhaps my head will come next, then my heart

I am caught in the past
only as long as my mind keeps me there

It's enough: those seven years together
These seven years of mourning

BOXES

My friend's mother tells me
ten years after her daughter's divorce
her daughter can't bear to go through the boxes
of belongings she once shared with her ex-fiancé
What are you going to do with bone china
in a one-room apartment? she says
I know how she feels
My boxes stay packed up too

Last week, visiting home in Boston
I was finally going to open them up
to sort through the old life I'd had with my ex:
boxes filled with photos of friends I hadn't seen in years,
hand towels in colors that matched my old bathroom,
and stationery imprinted with my old address

Instead, I spent the days processing my stillborn child
My book published, but unseen. Birthed, but broken
Hashing out my feelings of loss and wonder
I talked non-stop with my mother:
I was grateful that at the very least
I had written what I needed,
processed my fragmented life
and finally understood how those pieces fit together

Were it not for this stoppage—
this surprising umbilical strangulation—
I would not have come out of my sadness
to this place of understanding and self-knowing
I wouldn't have found my center, this place of compassion
I never would have truly understood mercy

For five years after my ex and I broke up
I couldn't unpack boxes
or put up a Christmas tree

This year, I put one up with my mother
The next time I'm home, we'll unpack my boxes
and give the things I no longer need or want, away

HEALING

Friday night
you flew into New York
Your old city, now mine

It had been seven years
since I'd last seen you
I'd forgotten you existed

Elegant, like Cary Grant in movies
You layered a black velvet sport coat
over trim jeans and Italian wingtips

You looked mostly the same
Perhaps, a bit more tired
The grind of life taking its toll

We talked until five
Weak from my cold
I went home to take my medicine

You built a stoop of regret
With slabs of longing
For memories of when we walked together

In that night air
Nothing could have shaded us

No waves of hope
Not the finest sombrero

FOUR: Men

SHELVED

I bought Diet Coke for Armen
Pancake mix, maple syrup and corn nuts for Tom
Brussel sprouts and lamb chops for Hernan
Edy's lime fruit bars for Ben

What I buy at the grocery store tells me
whether I really like a man or not
Anytime I do buy food for a man I'm dating
it usually means I won't be dating him very long

Those items, selected from grocery aisles
portending a recipe for disaster

On my shelves sit boxes of pancake mix
and bottles of maple syrup
My freezer is filled with key lime popsicles
Frozen meat and Brussels sprouts

RETRAINING

The new man I'm dating says
he and his wife froze their embryos
because she needed to preserve her child-bearing ability
before receiving cancer treatment. She didn't survive

On our date, he tells me he's not sure he'd ever use them,
but says the embryos still sit in a cryogenic freeze

He says at forty-one, I should freeze my eggs now
and buy myself time:
that a relationship needs to naturally unfold

He says, *of course* I'd want to have a baby
with a man I love, eventually
instead of with an anonymous sperm donor today

I can't imagine what purpose
my life would—or will ever—have
if I never bear any children

My cousin tells me she aborted hers because
although her boyfriend had money, he did drugs:
she'd just received her Ph.D. and gotten a new job

My other cousin tells me she loves babysitting
her friend's kids, but they're a lot of work. At forty-four,
she says she's not sorry she doesn't have one of her own

My mother, a doctor, says the Western culture we live in
doesn't value feminine traits
She says ambition and "left-brain" math-oriented skills
are what employers pay for here in the U.S.

All I'd ever wanted to do
was to be a wife and mother to the man I loved
and host my own cooking show on TV

Single and without children at forty-one
I wish I could take my colleague's advice
from fifteen years ago:
Don't fall in love in the first television market you work in
Don't fall in love with the place, or, with a man

Today, it's 2013 and I have no job
I have no husband or children:
the things I long for

Perhaps it's time for me to go back to school
where I might achieve a stable career
and make good money if, say, I were to become a nurse

I try to get my head around
taking entrance exams so I can
re-route myself in a more pragmatic direction

But for some things in life,
like learning to let go of the people you've loved,
there are no exams to take, and there is no retraining

NOT HAVING SEX

At the movies, we hold hands
Sit close together, our thighs touching
Me, in snug jeans
You, in your crisp khaki pants

When the previews start
you snake your arm through mine
You put my hand in your lap
Our shoulders touch, I rest my head on your neck,
swing my left leg over your right one

You wrap your right arm around my waist
Rub my back through my shirt
You sit forward so I can wrap my left arm
around your back, and I do

You unbutton your shirt two buttons deep
revealing a fresh white T-shirt
You place my hand over the T-shirt, on your chest
where your heart would be

You turn right and kiss me in the theatre's darkness
as the characters on-screen inch closer together

This is only our second date, after all
and we're not even going steady

BLOOD ORANGES AND A DISCO MIX TAPE

PART I

I guess I must really like him
since I deleted his number from my cell phone
the way I always do when I really like someone
so I won't drunk dial or text a man when I shouldn't

He found me online and sent me a note
I didn't respond the first time and he sent another email
I didn't think he was my type: blonde, blue-eyed, Southern
I hadn't picked up on the fact that we went to the same school

He said he'd come from Manhattan to meet me in Brooklyn
and asked me for my favorite spots
When I said my haunts were getting trite
He offered to pick a place instead

We shared *prosecco* at an Italian *trattoria*
He fed me blood orange and pomegranate seed salad
bathed in a lemony vinaigrette
We used SAT vocabulary words, rattled off witty exchanges
He said he liked how I used the word *cleaved*
to describe how a couple might be together

He told me he enjoyed cooking with his late wife
and that she'd graduated from Harvard the same year as me
He said they'd met at the business school
and asked me whether I knew some of her friends (yes)

There's something strangely comforting about dating someone
who lost someone they were in love with, so young
Her disease, terminal cancer
my ex's affliction, left undiagnosed

PART II

With Donna Summer playing on the radio
the lighting designer I'm also dating says
disco is the best and most underrated music

He promises to make me a disco mix tape
and says he just wants to be with a nice girl
Last night, I cancelled a tennis date with a man
who'd taken me out bowling once
He asked if I'd pay the seventy dollars for court time
since last time, he paid for bowling

My mother tells me she did everything for my father:
she helped him through college and law school,
cared for his children and family,
and it still wasn't enough

My therapist tells me sometimes
we have to teach ourselves to receive
That we have to train ourselves to learn
how to allow the kindness in

For twenty years I've given out love, thinking
it might translate into receiving kindness
The type of kindness that goes into making a disco mix tape:
a new CD, I have yet to play

LAST NIGHT'S KISS

You had soft lips, a warm tongue,
a wide smile, and a warm heart. I told you
you were unlike the men I'd dated in New York:
that while not becoming entirely jaded,
I'd essentially given up on dating—that everyone
in the City seemed to have another agenda—
but that you, from Princeton,
seemed genuine and sincere
At thirty-six, your maturity and focus surprised me

Already the father of three,
your divorce nearly two years old,
you confessed you had wanted to leave earlier—
not because you were angry—
but because you no longer felt alive
You said when you were first married,
you were always excited to see your wife
when she came home from work trips,
and that you hadn't wanted her to leave in the first place
You confessed that as the marriage went on
you were happier to just be alone with the kids
when work took her away

Last night, I didn't expect a kiss from you
We talked for five hours over nachos and beer
You told me about your hedge fund,
ultimate Frisbee league, penchant for working out,
playing tennis and listening to top-40 music
I rambled on about politics and books,
speculated on Hillary's presidential intentions in 2016
and how John Kerry would be a good Secretary of State

I asked to see photos of your three children
You seemed surprised, then pulled out your phone

Not long ago, I learned not to text or call after a date
to say *Thank you, I had a nice time,* even if I did
Knowing that if a man wants to,
he'll reach out on his own
Then you know for sure, he really does like you

You texted me this morning
I had a great time, have a good weekend away
With just a day between us, last night's kiss lingers
Tender, like the ones in old Jerry Vale songs

BREAKING NEWS

On hearing the news of the twenty children
shot dead by a crazed gunman
in a Connecticut elementary school
only an hour away from where I live in New York City
I am reminded of the beautiful photos
the man I went on a date last night showed me
of his amazing, vibrant and so-full-of-life children

I think of their faces:
Houston, Kayla and Aidan
at six, eight, and ten
Precocious and precious
it was he who said
They each have their own personality
but they're all showboats

He speaks of how he'd wanted children
since he was fifteen
and did have them, starting at twenty-six
He tells me he likes to spend money
on the people he loves
Shows me the picture of his daughter
sporting a scooter helmet shaped like a cat
wearing a tiara

He says to me how, on a holiday visit to his father's in Florida
he'll take the train instead of flying
He says it's a quirk his dad thinks he developed
only after he'd had children

I think of how, just two years ago—
while watching fathers and their kids play in Prospect Park—
it occurred to me, my idea of men was tainted
by my own experience with my father:
that I had a core belief that men only saw children
as a bother and intrusion—
as something to be dealt with, but not chosen

I realize how that kind of thinking
has limited the men I've chosen to date,
only leaving me open to the ones uninterested
in having children and being good dads

This morning, my mother tells me
she's happy to go to the fertility clinic with me
I finally made an appointment to explore my options
to bear my own child, single, at forty-one

This man I went on a date with last night
told me up front: should the woman
he were to fall in love with want her own family,
he'd do it all over again

I think of those families in Newtown, Connecticut
of the tiny bodies that still lay
in that kindergarten classroom, now a crime scene
even hours after the massacre

I think of the loss of being kept away from those babies
and of the rosy cheeks and toothy grins of my date's children

I imagine how tightly he will hug his kids tonight:
how much he'll tell them he loves them

I think of how risky it is to have a child
and how much my mother still worries about me

Despite today's unspeakable horror
I look forward to visiting the fertility clinic next week

To discover for myself, the joy wrapped inside
a soft pink or light blue blanket

FIVE: Possibility

FERTILITY CLINIC

At the fertility clinic, the doctor—
who's about my age—explains
there are two sperm banks:
one in Virginia, one in California
that are good to look into for donations
They used to cost fifty bucks, she says
Now, it's more like seven hundred

I ask if I could get a friend to donate. I have no partner
My previous relationship ended when I was thirty-five
I ask the doctor about freezing my eggs
She says it was only a few months ago,
in the summer of 2012, that egg freezing
was deemed a legitimate medical practice
that yielded healthy babies

My mother, also a doctor, nods when the doctor says
No, you wouldn't have known to freeze your eggs before now
She says at forty-one, my chances of having a baby are:
five to ten percent with regular insemination
twenty percent if you do IVF treatments with hormones

She does the ultrasound of my uterus
and shows me the picture of my ovarian follicles
She points out there are multiple pockets of eggs
and says *That's great news*

I take this to mean there's a better chance
that of my thousand or so remaining eggs
some are still viable for a healthy baby

Today, they draw blood and do some tests
My next appointment is in two weeks
I've asked my mother to leave Boston
and move here to New York
Alone, I could not raise this child

If your partner is your parent, is that so wrong?
It is, after all, how she raised me

I AM NOT A VIRGIN

I am not a virgin,
although like all women
I was once
This Christmas, however
I hope to become more like the Virgin Mary

I'll never be able to reclaim my purity
since there are some things that can't be changed
But I would welcome a new type of virgin birth
or miracle child: a baby Jesus of my own
Perhaps that's what IVF, sperm
and egg donors are today:
acts of God yielding gifts
no-one would have believed possible before

As I make the appointment with the fertility clinic
and tell my mother and friends
at forty-one, I'm ready to have a child,
I know it's no longer Joseph I seek

Growing up, my mother would say
to look to the North Star, should I ever get lost
I seek it now, its clarion guidance
and pray for it to light me a new way home

TAKING SIDES

My left breast is bigger than my right one
My right foot is wider than my left one

My right eyebrow arches higher than my left one
The hair on the left side of my head is longer than the hair on the right

Each month, an egg drops from my left or right ovary
One at a time, they descend, hoping to make more of themselves

Instead, they are flushed out, let go of, and passed on
All sides hear the sound of time winding down

Tick tock, tick tock

A POEM ABOUT VIOLENCE

PART I

I read the article in *The New York Times*
about the forty-four year old mother of a six-month-old baby
who worked as an attorney in New York City
making a hundred and twenty-two thousand dollars a year
How she went to Columbia law school,
worked on women's rights in Pakistan
and how, long before she married her husband,
she bought her own apartment on 147th street in Harlem

How she was taking a break
from her high-pressured job
to care for her newborn son, when
in a thirteen-page scripted note
she says she felt it was her fault he'd slipped
and bumped his head once or twice
and as a result, she thought he'd end up
with some kind of disfigurement or disease

The article then says
she put on her Ergobaby carrier, strapped him in,
and dove off the eighth floor of her apartment
In her thirteen-page note, she said
she felt it was a better fate for them both
because she couldn't live with herself
for causing the child harm

Except the child wasn't harmed then
and he wasn't harmed when she jumped
Although the woman did die upon impact
her body protected the baby
Her son bounced out of the baby carrier
and escaped, the article noted,
with only with a bruise on his cheek

The newspaper reporter says,
when contacted by phone at home,
the father said he was overwhelmed by grief
but lucky to be holding his son in his lap

The reporter noted, that in fact,
a child's whimpers could be heard
on the other end of the line

PART II

It's the end of the first week
where I'm once again unemployed
Management cut the newscasts I anchored
at the TV station, *for budgetary reasons,* they said

My mother visited me for a week
in my rented Brooklyn apartment
for moral support, she said
She did my laundry
We watched Roger Federer play tennis on TV
We took long walks in Prospect Park

On those walks, I explained
I was glad I was choosing better men to date:
ones that were kinder and more mature
I also explained that because I was once again unemployed
I couldn't see myself going forward with my original plan
to have a baby through a sperm donor at the fertility clinic
if one of these men didn't work out
(Because who in their right mind would try to have a child
when they didn't even have an income)

PART III

Reading the article about the mother
who strapped her baby to her chest
before jumping to her death
I think about all the good she had going for her:
a husband, a high-earning attorney job
a son and an apartment she owned in Manhattan

All the things I wish I had going for me, I don't have:
the things I say I want

My single girlfriend who works on Wall Street
and also owns her own apartment in New York City
tells me I need to be grateful for what I do have
and not envy others, because after all, who knows
what people's lives are really like behind closed doors

I think of all the alcohol I've ingested, the cigarettes,
the fatty foods: the ways I chip away at my well-being

My life hasn't turned out the way I'd hoped or expected it would
But for some reason, I continue to honor it by living

SIX: Awakening

PICTURE OF ME

I see myself at four or five years old
sitting in a white rubber room
My hair is parted down the middle
held with *bolitas*—pony tail holders
My hair is styled in my grandmother's ringlets
and sits atop my left and right shoulders

In that room, with a bright light shining in
from one high corner window, I am naked
I am alone, I am crying
I am screaming and looking for help

Sitting in my own pool of feces and urine
I am afraid and lonely
I've been by myself for so long
with no-one to care for me
I see a huge door with a small window
It's much too big for me to open

My therapist says to have the adult me
look at that child, open the door
pick her up and hold her close

To hum in her ear and tell her
Everything's going to be all right
To give her a hug
To give her a bath
To change her into a new pink dress

When I open the door to that boxed room,
that all-white rubber room,
I see my five-year-old self sitting
in that mess of her own pee and poop

I grab her
Squeeze her little body hard
Hold her tight
Smooth her dark hair
I give her a bath
I change her into fresh clothes
I give her something to eat and to drink

I hug her again
I tell her she is loved
That she's a precious, amazing child

I sing to her. I say
I'll always be with you
I will protect you
I will never leave

ROOTED

I am rooted in my own body
I am calling home to me
My five foot eight inch frame
My one hundred and eighty-five pounds

I'm rooted in my sturdy legs
my large feet, my curled toes
Home is where the heart is, they say
Home, finally more than where I hang my hat

Papa was a rolling stone and I learned to roll, too,
through jobs in Ohio, Connecticut, Pennsylvania
Massachusetts, Florida, Upstate New York
and now, New York City

I've lived here nearly four years
in this city of over eight million
I've lived here longer than anywhere else in my adult life:
longer than I ever thought I'd stay

It took me coming to this enormous city
filled with people from neighboring New Jersey,
Trinidad and the Ukraine, to take the time to sit
and learn myself: the endless pavement
and parade of strangers was at first too much for me

Instead, I sat in my Brooklyn studio with my kitty Louisa
and dug out all the things I couldn't stand about me:
the things I knew made me a bad person
and made me feel ashamed
Things I never spoke of
Things that had no name

Rooting myself, to myself
lawn grubs, be gone

Tall and elegant like birch
Thick and strong like oak
Bending, like the willow

BITING MY NAILS

When I stopped biting my nails
I started chewing gum

When I stopped chewing gum
I started eating oatmeal, popcorn and pasta

When I stopped eating carbs
I started cheating at school

When I stopped cheating at school
I started driving too fast

When I stopped driving too fast
I started smoking cigarettes

When I stopped smoking cigarettes
I started drinking wine

When I stopped drinking wine
I started padding my expense reports

When I stopped padding my expense reports
I started sniping at my mother and fiancé

When I stopped sniping at my loved ones,
I stopped

When I stopped sniping at myself,
I stopped

When I stopped,
I stopped

Suddenly, all fell silent
Suddenly, all was good

THE SPINSTER

My mother, who never slept with anyone but my father
who she married two weeks before my birth,
has been asked on more than one occasion
whether she was a lesbian

Of course, anyone who knows my mother—
an Emergency Room physician
with her Master's in Public Health who yes,
wears her hair shorter now that she's seventy-two
and has, for at least a decade—
knows she does it merely out of convenience
She also prefers comfortable, sturdy clothes to fancy,
save for when a special occasion
warrants a Black Tie-kind of outfit
Then, her regal class is tough to touch

Many have asked why she never dated after my father
She'd say it's because she didn't trust herself with men
and because, as the oldest child of five
she had other responsibilities:
her work with the poor
her political causes seeking justice
caring for her aging parents
looking after her siblings financially and emotionally
raising her daughter—me
and countless other activities she chose to take on

At seventy-two, I doubt my mother longs or longed for a man
After my father, whom she recently admitted
was an emotional terrorist,
she was just happy to escape his rage

As I sit here making turkey chili
in my studio apartment in Brooklyn:
candles lit, a glass of red wine,
my kitty Louisa by my side resting quietly,
I wonder if—at forty-one—this will be my life
and whether I'd even be at all sad if it were

Before, I could never escape my longing for a man
I'd made countless desperate attempts
at companionship and seeking fulfillment:
a need that now, has simply evaporated

It's not that I don't like or enjoy men, or people
It's not because I don't want a child of my own—
biological preferred—someday soon
It's simply because my need for a man has been erased

Chili, candles, red wine, LouisaKitty
Men may mock me, and women, too

But this graceful peace, this quiet space
gives me something others have not:
a comfort of my own
One that's more than enough

CONFIDENCE

People often tell me they think of me as confident
They say I hold my head high, think well of myself
and generally don't doubt what my life is about
They say I have a glamorous life, being single
and on TV in New York City
They see a certain part of me

So many times
I have doubted every single thing about me,
like today when I was happy to learn
my friend's bathroom had a skinny mirror
that made me look thinner than I actually am

Putting on concealer and mascara
I wondered if I'd end up crying today in poetry class
I didn't know that I would, so I put it on anyway,
thinking it's better to look and present well when I can:
I wore new jeans instead of my sweats
(There are other people in the class, after all)

Still, every day I look in the mirror
I see more of what time brings
Darker circles under my eyes, little brown spots
Blemishes on my chin from adult acne
Thinning hair that's been falling out in clumps

There was a time only a few months ago
when I truly felt happy
I accepted myself, didn't worry too much
about what other people thought
I was grateful for my job, my tiny apartment
my kitty Louisa and the people who loved me

But something's shifted back
to that place of not-knowing
If I'll really be OK
If I'll ever find true love
If I'll ever not need anyone

Today, I paint on a smile with lipstick
Make small talk about Caribbean island vacations
Wear tall black suede boots with brass zippers
to deflect others' eyes, from mine

WHAT SHE SAYS
- for Laura

She says
You're so original
You're so fresh
You're so daring
You're so unafraid

You're so resilient
You're so honest
You're so open
You're so brave

She says
You're so kind
You're so talented
You're so progressive
You're so good

She says
all the things someone
should say to her
and should have said to her
All the things, I should say

I AM NEW YORK

I've only lived here since 2009
but New York's the only place I've ever felt at home
save for when I was a student at Harvard
and my friends included Dutch fencing champions
as well as poor kids from Appalachia
and mixed race kids from the suburbs, like me

New York City, where did you come from?
You courted me and swept me off my feet
I wasn't ready for this kind of relationship
I didn't want to be faithful
It took me over three years to love you
You're the longest relationship I've ever had
(I even had to leave Harvard after two years
What was I doing there, anyway?
I went to Italy to write for travel guides, but came back)

I lived in Ohio for a year
Back in Boston for two
Then Binghamton for one
Then Syracuse for one and a half
Then Boston for one
Then Hartford for one
Then back to Boston for one
Then Hartford for one more
Then Binghamton for two
(where I thought I'd stay forever)
Then Florida for two
(after the economy crashed)

To New York, God himself came calling
in the form of a new Catholic TV station
They asked me to Anchor the newsmagazine, *Currents*
Although I'd seriously considered starting
my own media consulting business in Boston, I agreed

I came to Brooklyn, this amoeba-like place
filled with Russians, Chinese and West Indians
Every day, I see men dressed in Muslim or Hebrew garb
praying, or taking their kids to Prospect Park to play

I see forty year-old White men, pushing baby strollers
while Black nannies push other fair-skinned kids by
I'm Haitian-Dominican and Italian–American
I call myself Latalian for good reason
(I've learned self-definition is useful)

But like my mother's move
to be a doctor in the 1960's
I may have been, perhaps unknowingly
a bit ahead of my time

Not because of my career aspirations
but because I was confounded by my mixed race
It never seemed to occur to anyone that even with
the educational and social privileges afforded to me,
my ethnicity (and having a crazy father)
might also be an issue

Harvard Square felt like a warm bath, like coming home:
a place where everyone I knew was smart and different
Brooklyn and New York are that to me now
(and sure, boneheads still abound, as they do anywhere)

It took me three years
to love you, New York
Your hard cement, shiny towers
dog poop, and lack of grass

It took me three years to realize I love you
This home, I'll never leave

AT THE FLOWER MARKET IN BROOKLYN

I spy orange gerbera daisies
the color of fiery sunsets over the Hudson
Fuchsia flowers blend in like purple stratus clouds
Pale pink ones pop us, the color of a newborn's skin

Their tubular green stems
all xylem and phloem
propped up by a wide plastic straw
encircling delicate and nearly-hollow rods

Not propped up at sixty-eight is my best friend's mother
Once a wealthy agronomist in South America,
she sold roses, daisies and tulips around the world:
she knew the seasons, the soil, the markets

When the Florida housing market crashed in 2008,
her house was underwater. She lost it

That home, like so many others,
lost in a flood of hope and bad credit
This economy, no longer sunny
as her flower market once was

One where she traded orange gerbera daisies with ease
One with flowers that shone as brightly as the Colombian sun

GOING GREEN

When I moved to the Florida Panhandle in 2006
to anchor the news at the local ABC station
they called the area the Redneck Riviera
Being from Boston, I was surprised to learn Pensacola
had no curbside recycling program

I visited the county dump to ask why
I had several meetings with sanitation workers
They said they'd tried one program before
but that people didn't like having someone tell them what to do
They also said the way the system was structured back then,
it would cost more to recycle than bury waste in an Alabama landfill

When I joined the Pensacola Young Professionals
I began meeting with politicians and residents
We gathered at my house, watched *An Inconvenient Truth*
We visited City Council members and local company presidents

With people in their twenties and thirties lobbying hard,
the question was brought to the polls, where it got voted in

It's been six years since I left Pensacola
The curbside recycling program there still exists

In 2010 the BP Oil Spill nearly wiped out
the Kemp's ridley sea turtle population

They've resumed deep offshore drilling in the Gulf
Hatching progress doesn't come easy

SEVEN: Childhood

THE HAIRDRESSER

PART I

Now, they're called "stylists"
but you always said you were a hairdresser
You did hair for forty-five years,
until at seventy-five you didn't want to anymore

That's how you met my mother
You gave her a perm when she was twelve
You were thirteen years her senior
but are now of the "same generation"
Growing up, after union construction work, your husband Henry
worked masonry jobs with my Grandfather Louie
They built chimneys, slate walkways and pool patios
for non-Italians who could afford them. Piccioli, Magnani:
short Henry was a great fit for my thick Grampa
They were an Abbott and Costello kind of pair

You, Alba, I remember always in that yellow kitchen, cooking
surrounded by sunny, bright sunflower wallpaper
you said you put up yourself, because although
Henry was good at some things, like washing cars
he wasn't so good at finishing projects he'd started
Like when you painted the upper half of the kitchen
(the bottom half was the wallpaper)
and by the time you'd rung around the room
he was still slathering buttercream paint on the same wall

That yellow kitchen, its warm smells
Your peach cobbler, your rump roasts, your bacon and eggs
on Sundays, your cheesecakes. You gave me your recipes:
you knew I loved to cook and make blueberry muffins
When Henry died of a brain aneurysm at fifty-five,
now alone, you let me stay at your house overnight
while my mother worked as a doctor in the emergency room
You made me bacon and eggs, or fresh waffles for breakfast,
even school days

On Sundays my Grampa would take me by your house
He'd bring homemade cherry rum, garden tomatoes and zucchini
You'd be serving shepherd's pie, glazed carrots and green beans
to your three children, their wives and your grandchildren
I loved going there after mass at St. Cecelia's
where Grampa sung in the choir
Just one street, Main Street, stood between
Esty Street where the church was
and Clark Street where you lived

Unlike my grandparents who are now gone,
at eighty-five, you're still the center of Ashland
On one corner, the American Legion
On the other, Matarese's funeral home

PART II

You were the mother in so many ways I wish I'd always had
Yet, just as my mother's stepchildren betrayed her,
your biological children and grandchildren betrayed you

You didn't believe in going to therapy
and didn't fuss about getting into college
the way my mother did with me
Your main concern was whether someone was happy
You worked hard and kept your kitchen spotless:
the smell of freshly-made coffee
in the countertop percolator still fills my nostrils

You raised your oldest son's
two biracial daughters as your own,
with their own mini cupcake pans
and artists easels in the basement
You found a way to braid and tame their unruly locks
You even roller set mine for my Junior Prom

You were always glowing; so petite and perky,
that strawberry blonde hair coiffed
in a thoroughly modern shorter, upswept cut:
unfussy, bold, and feminine at the same time

You, tan and bronzed
from Saturdays spent on the lounger by the grape arbor
You, who wore royal blue and jade green dresses
and danced every weekend with Henry
at the VFW and the Knights of Columbus
You, who washed more heads and gave tighter perms
than anyone else at Josephine's hairdressing shop in Natick
You, who still took calls from your old customers
(they weren't called "clients" then) even after you retired:
I don't remember those ladies' names,
but I remember that as you learned one of them had passed,
you'd get tears in your eyes, knowing they were gone

PART III

After your husband Henry died
your oldest son said you'd become a bitter old woman
After all you'd done for his family
you were stunned by his declaration,
but were still willing to let them go

Alba, I long for the days I smell peach cobbler,
sip tea in your kitchen
and share things no-one wants to acknowledge or say

I long for when I can come home to celebrate
the victory of your eighty-five years, in that kitchen:
one to me, that will forever be sunny, warm, and bright

PINOCCHIO

My grandfather always made me a Pinocchio nose

In the mornings before school, and sometimes after work, too, he'd use the white ceramic cup with the hockey-puck-sized scented soap in it, and take the bristly brush, run it under a hot tap, and swirl it around in circles until it made a nice, thick, foamy lather not unlike the meringue I'd later learn to make for lemon pies

He'd look up in the mirror and start at the base of his neck around his Adam's apple, and move up

In that small kitchen off the dining room, under the fluorescent lights, he'd create white swirls on his stubbly neck, forming nautilus shells like the patterns from 1970's plaster ceilings... painting his own face, making funny faces as he drew his upper lip down over his teeth to mark off his moustache, then pulling his lower lip up over his teeth, in a Bobby De Niro-like way, to get a better protruding chin

He always used simple, plastic Bic razors, the yellow ones you'd buy with ten or twelve in a pack. No straight razor for him, although I know he used to have one when he was younger: I remember the leather strap used for sharpening it, hanging in the kitchen

I loved the fresh, clean smell of that soap and of knowing Grampa was home. Of knowing he was doing what he always did. Of there being a routine he shared with me

He often had to mix more of the lathery-soap, and when it was 'just right,' just like a batch of the mortar he'd mix for his masonry jobs— not too wet or too dry—he'd dollop an index-finger's worth of lather right on the end of my nose

I'd smile when he did it: that fresh-smelling clean soap, now right on top of my own nose. At six or seven, he'd pick me up, and with my curls or pigtails, he'd hold me straight in front of the mirror, so I could see this white Pinocchio nose he'd adorned me with

I never could stop grinning. I was so proud to share these moments with Grampa. So lucky to have this special ritual. So grateful for our time

When the sound of his shave had run dry, he'd towel off, and top it off with Old Spice. He'd shake it onto the palms of his wide, calloused hands, patting each side of his thick, strong neck. The smell of that cologne became synonymous with him for me, just as my mother's Shalimar was, for her

When I heard him release the sink's lock from left to right, and heard the water begin to drain, I knew that our time was up: that he was cleaned up and ready to go

Like the tiny pieces of my Grandfather's stubble that clung in a ring around the wall of the small bathroom sink after he'd shaved, I cling to those memories, to those safe rituals, to that Pinocchio nose

I NEVER LIKED CARNIVALS

Carnivals are frowning clown faces:
a wide upside-down smile on a ceramic head
with big red lips outlined in white
That frizzy orange hair, the satin harlequin suit
The crazed look in painted-on eyes

I never liked roller coasters or cotton candy
I was never especially good at shooting the water
into the mouth of a moving rubber duck
for a teddy bear prize

I didn't like the heat the carnivals came with
Didn't like the dusty summer air
that baked into my skin when I'd rather be swimming
I didn't like the idea of paying for rides in teacups
I found the Ferris wheel boring
(I never had a boyfriend to go out and hold hands with,
which might have made the slow ride to the top more fun)

I didn't mind when the ride operator measured my height
because I didn't mind being as tall as I was,
but I dreaded getting on a scale in front of other people
to determine my weight because of limits on certain rides

When those fairs would roll into my neighboring town
and all the kids from school wanted to go
it was a reminder of how not normal I was:
how public school was not for me, and how those kids
who enjoyed carnivals, weren't the ones
who'd become my lifelong friends

Only when my grandfather took me
did I ever enjoy the creaky rides and heavy air

Not because we were at the carnival
but because he was anything but a clown, to me

HAUNTED HOUSE

In Philadelphia, soon after my ex and I had broken up
I got a reporting assignment
to cover a haunted house for Halloween

I was thin at the time and never enjoyed being scared
I wasn't yet highly skilled at structuring my stories,
even though I'd been hired to work
in a TV market of four million people
when just two years before, I'd been in Binghamton
with only two hundred thousand

That haunted house,
with its musty smell and creaky sounds,
had people coming out of crevices
and covered windows to surprise me
It wasn't unlike when someone comes up
from behind me at my desk now,
or when the elevator opens
and I jump back when I find someone already inside

I'm not someone normally scared
of things like spiders or heights
I overcame my fear of sharks
by getting my SCUBA license in the Gulf of Mexico

Still, I'll never be a fan of a haunted house:
of those fabricated, scary moments
meant to shock you into feeling alive

No, my life has had plenty of those already, including
my ex breaking up with me two days before our wedding
and someone who didn't like my book, threatening fallout

While I couldn't eat for a week after both of those events
and lost ten pounds each time
I wouldn't wish those kinds of surprises on anyone:
the high price of admission, for going inside

80's TV

I used to watch
Welcome Back Kotter and *Happy Days*
Laverne and Shirley, Three's Company
Too Close for Comfort
The Beverly Hillbillies
Lawrence Welk
Gimme a Break!
The Golden Girls

Those were the shows I watched with Grama
at my grandparents house
when my mom was at work and my Grampa was out
and I was supposed to be doing my homework
or practicing my ballet, tap or jazz steps, or the piano

Unlike my mother, who encouraged me to eat cucumbers
and green beans, make salads and drink seltzer water with lime
Grama let me eat Pecan Sandies and drink orange juice
She kept Chips Ahoy and Uneeda Biscuits in her house for snacks

Those times were different
from when my mother let my father's kids—
my half-siblings—come visit on weekends
at the apartment I shared with my mother
There, we watched *Dallas, Falcon Crest*
Fantasy Island, Dukes of Hazard
During those shows, my half-siblings found ways
to provoke, tease and scare me
the way I'm told full siblings often also do

I wished I remained without any siblings
although I did want more friends to play with, growing up
When I told my mother I was lonely, she said
Are you lonely, or just alone
She felt compelled to switch me from Montessori—
where there were only three girls my age—to public school
Her sense of obligation, also compelling her to bring
unwanted strangers into our home for my company
even when I would have preferred to remain an only child

GOOD TIMES

I can hear the song now:
Good Times. These are the good times
Leave your cares behind. These are the good times

Perhaps those were the good times:
when I'd be at my father's house listening to
the Gap Band and Peaches & Herb
Cameo, Prince, the Bee Gees
Sister Sledge, and of course, Chic

Perhaps those were the good times:
impromptu dance lessons, practicing the snake
watching MTV, trying to be Paula Abdul and Janet Jackson,
wondering why my hair wasn't in Jeri curls or corn rows

Visiting my father, everyone around me had brown skin
while mine remained olive, except in summertime
when I'd windsurf or sail at Hopkinton State Park:
by September, I became bronzed

Those people surrounding my father spoke in tongues
I didn't understand: ones I didn't want to learn
My Italian-American mother told me to pragmatically
take Spanish as a foreign language in High School
But I refused, not wanting to associate in any way
with my father and his wrath

He was Haitian-Dominican and spoke proper French
but his main language was actually Creole
Even though his mother, whom I loved,
spoke almost entirely in Spanish, I refused to learn it well

Most Italians I know have a story, as my grandfather did,
of them not being taught Italian
because their parents who came over on Ellis Island
wanted them to be American

They didn't want there to be another stigma against them
even though today, my Iranian friend in New York City
married a Bolivian and has her three daughters
speaking and reading English, Spanish and Farsi

Shame has no language, other than the cowardice of self-rejection
I wish I'd had more good times with my father to fondly remember
Instead, vivid childhood memories of his terror remain

When I hear those boom box beats of blackness on the radio
I'm reminded of the cloak of Spanish we share: one I'll never shed

When those songs play in my head, even in summertime,
I find myself shopping for sweaters spun on Italian looms

MY REAL NAME

My real name is Frances, not Francesca
My mother named me after my first cousin
and St. Francis of Assisi
I unofficially changed it in college
after working in Italy one summer
The new name suited me and gave me a new self
free of tangled Hispanic roots

Today, when I visit the bookstore,
I see children's books titled:
"Does Anybody Else Look Like Me?
A Parent' Guide to raising Multiracial Children"
"Of Many Colors: Portraits of Multiracial Families"
and, *"All Kinds of People"*

In 2012, adults I've spoken to say
It's really about how you self-identify
(unless, of course, you're visibly black,
then you're stuck, in some ways,
with how the world perceives you)

So I'll keep the *accent aigu*
on my Haitian last name, Maximé
(it's always a conversation-starter)
I'll add the extra "ca" on my first name, because I can
While part Dominican, I never learned Spanish well,
even though Hispanics
are the fastest-growing population in the U.S.
(Not knowing the language didn't help my career
when CNN called to cover Barack Obama's inauguration
because they thought I was bilingual)

My real name, like me in so many ways,
remains a mix and mystery
rooted in Caribbean island sand, African slaves
Italian peasants and Arab Moors from Spain

MY GRANDMOTHER SENDS ME SILKY NIGHTGOWNS

My grandmother would always send me
boxes of silky nightgowns
The kind you might expect someone to buy
if they were going on their honeymoon
but shopped at Woolworth's

They weren't the Laura Ashley flannels
I'd grown up with in New England
They were pearly white, ecru, pink and mint green
Light blue with thin lace, peach with short sleeves
Yellow with a matching half-robe

I never quite understood why my grandmother
who, in the same care package, might also send
fried chicken or fried plantains (*platanos*), would,
as a divorced mother of six who feared God so much
consider these appropriate for a child of eight, nine or ten

I know she knew I lived alone with my mother
and so, it's not like there was anyone else
in the house who'd see me

And I know she wasn't trying to make me
into some kind of sexual being, because
she herself was always my champion and protector

Still, I wonder if she just thought
these pink and lace nylon gowns were pretty
That they were something nice, something sweet:
something she could do for me, from across the miles

I wonder if she wishes she'd had them
when she was a young girl,
to feel beautiful, and cared for

I wonder what she'd have done
if someone had thought as much of her
when she was my age, as she had thought of me

THINGS MY FATHER USED TO EAT

Looking at the bag of *turbinado* pure cane sugar
I bought at the Dominican supermarket
in my Brooklyn neighborhood
I am reminded of the strange things
my father used to eat in Chicago when I was a child

Octopus: maroon and dark purple
with white suckers and long, gangly tentacles
Cow's tongue or beef tongue
(which you can also find at my Dominican market
along with chicken's feet, cow intestines, and pig's feet)

He would gorge himself on red rice and beans
chicken with saffron and *carne asada*

Sometimes he'd bring home a fresh sugar cane
long and bamboo-like, but wider, and slice it open
Raw and juicy, with its sweet blood pouring out,
we'd tear in, chew at it, and suck it bone dry

My mother tells the story of when he and his Indian friend
once ate pickled mangoes so hot and spicy, sweat poured
off their brows onto their plates, as they sucked them down
They relished the fire on their tongues

There is a picture of me in my pajamas
with my father holding me when I was a child
He's also holding a can of beer
There's fried chicken in a box on the table

I asked him for *A little bit of beer, Papi*
He let me sip it, at two years old
I don't know who took that picture
although I suspect my mother did

Sitting on my father's lap that day
was as close to him as I ever got
I'll always crave that sweetness
Gritty, like raw sugarcane

SHAME

Shame hung over the Massachusetts apartment I grew up in
the same way the sun shone over the sparkling blue water
when I'd leave my apartment in Pensacola, Florida
to go play tennis before I started work at two P.M.

In my childhood apartment, it was always there:
In invisible clouds that hung low
In the dust particles and cat hair
In the creaky crevices of the second floor bedrooms
In the mold that grew in the corners of the damp basement
In the candle wax that dripped from the coffee table
and was stuck on the green paisley-patterned linoleum floor

It was in the toxic fumes of Easy Off my mother would use
to clean the oven after cooking the Christmas turkey
and even in the Shalimar she'd put on for the family dinner
before that turkey was cooked
It was in the white rubber girdle I wore in fifth grade
to suck in my thighs and rear-end
before I put on my flowered skirt to wear to school
while everyone else wore sleek Jordache jeans

It was in the Nivea cream my mother used
to smooth out my kinky hair before braiding it tight
(There were no products for Haitian-Dominican Italian
kids like me. Now they have serums for so-called
"Mixed Chicks." Apparently, we've come a long way)

Or have we? Because shame still hangs in the
film covering the mirrors in my New York City apartment
Its in the makeup sponges soaked in pigment I use
to paint my face free of blemishes before I anchor the news
It's in the way I often wobble wearing five-inch heels
despite my size ten feet and hundred and eighty-five pound frame

It grew from that Ashland, Massachusetts apartment I grew up in,
out of the floorboards, and sank right into my feet
It grounded me, seeping into my pores
like the smell of my mother's spaghetti sauce, simmering

106

It's found its way here to New York City now, too
Thirty years later, it still finds its way into me
through those microscopic semi-permeable membranes:
ones unsure of what to let in and what to keep out

LEGITIMATE

I used to love going shopping
because I thought
buying a new pair of shoes
would make me look legitimate

Those pink high-heeled pumps
with the rose bow on top,
a ticket to fancy and sexy:
to being wanted and want-able

A good Italian leather purse meant I had class
A dress with the right fit and fine fabric
like wool gabardine, if nipped in the waist,
would somehow disguise my hips and thighs
and make me appear smaller than I really was

I scoured the racks at TJ Maxx, Marshalls
and Filene's Basement for quality finds
I once bought a pair of gold slingbacks
at Building 19 for fifty dollars made by
Susan Bennis and Warren Edwards
My fashionable friend from New York City
noticed them right away
He called out the brand name,
exclaiming that his sister just bought
a similar pair at Bergdorf's
for three hundred and fifty dollars

I think of how the kitchen my ex and I built—
with its Viking stove and Sub-Zero refrigerator,
green Murano pendant lights
and granite countertops—
how those were currency. Each item,
a little stack of legitimacy I could display

Just like my fiancé himself:
six foot two, college educated
well-off, handsome and cultured
With him, I automatically felt more legitimate
just like my job on TV makes me feel today

Still, after trying to go without them,
I've had long my hair extensions put back in
I shop for MAC makeup in complimentary colors
For new jeans that cost hundreds, but fit me well

I used to buy these things
because they made me feel more acceptable:
they removed the shame I felt inside

Today my worth isn't measured
by a pair of shoes or a handsome fiancé

Legitimacy, I give myself
My dignity, no longer for sale

OH.MY.GOD.

Perhaps my problem is there are no more OMG moments

I've written about my obsession with food
My cracking up cars
My drinking too much
My dating too many boys

I've written about my troubled relationship
with my abusive father
The way I do and don't like the way my ass looks
in a pair of jeans
I've already written about the way I used to
pad my expense reports and how I resigned because of it
I've told people the story of how I sometimes
cheated in high school, to get into a good college

I've already said that although I didn't know
he was married at the time (he'd lied to me about it)
that I'd been with a married man
I thought I was actually dating

I've told my mother I was mad at her for bringing my
half-siblings into our home when they weren't her children
I've told her I wished she would have
protected me more from my father's abusive behavior

I've admitted I could have been nicer to my ex-fiancé
and that my sniping about what he didn't do right
(like stick up for me in front of his father)
was likely a big part of that relationship's demise

I've come to terms with the fact that at forty-one
I may never have biological children,
but I've begun to explore sperm donation
and admitted I may not need or want a man
before trying to have kids

I've said nearly all there is to say
including how, in nervous anxiety
I'd pick at my face with tweezers, then use makeup
to cover the wounds before I went on TV

How I still find it difficult to have full compassion
for people who harbor evil thoughts
or towards those who were given chances at therapy,
decided against it, and now have troubled children

I have come to accept myself
Curves and all—my new me
I accept that I wear hair extensions and use makeup
to keep me looking as young as I once appeared naturally

I accept the fact that my life is what it is,
and for that, I'm grateful:
this self-awareness, brought to me
by tunneling through my childhood

A childhood constructed of thick concrete blocks
as rough and heavy
as the ones my grandfather
easily held two of, in each hand

EIGHT: Boundaries

SUICIDE NOTE

PART I

When he saw my father for the last time
He left the note on the kitchen table
saying that he had been a good father
(Which was a bit strange, since he is not his
father. But this is a suicide note of sorts,
after all, so there is room for poetic license)

PART II

The convicted felon in Webster, New York who lured
firefighters into his burning home in an ambush
before killing them with a Bushmaster rifle
left a suicide note, saying
he was doing what he did best: killing people
(Because he'd already done that before
by strangling his own grandmother to
death, eighteen years earlier)

PART III

We want to believe people
can automatically change with time's passage
or, because their life's circumstances have improved
But there are some people,
who simply are what they are

It was said to me not long ago:
When people show you who they are,
believe them the first time

Growing up, my grandmother would tell me:
Watch what people do, not what they say

On the phone, my great-aunt says my grandmother
always wanted to believe the best in people,
even if they've already played their hand

CINDERELLA COMES TO LIFE AT RICHARD BLANCO's APOCRYPHAL POETRY WORKSHOP

I imagine Cinderella not with a broom and long blond locks, but with dark hair like mine, a laptop computer by her side, writing, writing, writing her way into the night, rising in early mornings, looking outside of her bedroom window with the soft, cool rain falling on the birch and elm

Home alone, unharried by her evil stepsisters: those redheads who weigh too much and yell too much and who are always wanting more from her, who instead are the ones who live in the barn and who spend their time toiling after the horses, baling the hay, milking the cows and feeding the sheep

Cinderella writes about her love not of Prince Charming, but of life. She needs no ruby or glass slippers. She need not be Jennifer Lopez or Beyoncé, sporting two thousand dollar Christian Louboutins stamped with scarlet soles

No, this simple Cinderella prefers the warm comfort of shearling slippers. She longs not for a pumpkin carriage ride, merely for a driver who'll help her get from here to there: the vehicle in which she travels, less important than being entrusted to someone who mitigates her chances of being pulled over by a State Trooper, which happened once when she lost focus on her speed, and her thoughts were instead consumed by her stepsisters

Cinderella was shocked to learn they'd get a room inside the house. She was shocked to learn she'd have to share her bedroom: that the window she stared out from in solitude and peace, would be shattered with their cackles and shrieks in the morning as they commented on Cinderella's long, lush velvety brown locks: how the praised heaped on her by others for her elegance and beauty would be turned into venomous poison against her, and how she learned to have to wear a *hijab* instead

Miss Cinderella shared that space, shared the house. She even gave these stepsisters an extra key, should they ever get locked out. This was her obligation to others, her family training really: her ability to see that they too, were wounded and had endured a hard life toiling in the fields

She longed for the day they might live in peace: when they could play jacks together, Sorry or Boggle, Crazy 8's or even Rummy 500

But no, those days were not to be: instead, while watching *Fantasy Island,* Cinderella's stepsisters surprised her with a creepy sound as the program entered the fantasy land where the half-man half-goat walked through the maze. Cinderella, frightened by this creature, and even more so after her stepsisters jumped up behind her, creating such a fright, was unable to sleep

Instead, she tossed and turned like the Princess and the Pea. Unable to rest, unable to get rest, she continued like this, day, after day. Nights became longer, sleep became scarce, her inner self withered: Mrs. Cinderella Dorian Gray

Her long locks started falling out, her computer, abandoned and dusty, the windows, plastered closed. The red velvet curtains, drawn shut

Seeking strength, Cinderella crept toward the pantry for some sustenance, only to find her stepsisters had eaten all the food in the cupboard; the shelves bare of anything she could ingest

Seeking basic nutrition for survival, Cinderella went searching in the fields for something she could find to satisfy her craving: for some way to make sense out of what had happened to her life

She alternatively longed for the days she'd stare out of her window, writing in quiet solitude, her satisfaction and safety complete, and for the triumph she knew she would achieve, on this day, as she found the berries she sought in the woods and ate them: the fresh, juicy, dark-hued luscious fruit. This natural sustenance, enough to carry her forward: enough to make her march on

CHRISTMAS WITH LOUISA

It is Christmas 2011 and it's the worst one yet
I'm spending it in the basement with my cat Louisa
She's the only one I want to see

Who are all these people in my house?
Why are they all here?
Where'd the other ones like Grampa, go?

Aunt Rachel, buried this year and her husband
already spending Christmas in North Carolina
with his new girlfriend's deceased husband's family

One relative comes with her new fiancé and his child
My cousin, with her boyfriend
My other cousin, with his girlfriend and her son

I say take Christmas, because my mom's seventy-one
She's done this for thirty-nine years
and doesn't feel like doing it anymore
Still, there was all that work she put into:

Cleaning the house and decorating the tree
Shopping for the turkey and scallops and salad:
how she roasted the two kinds of rosemary potatoes,
served the shrimp cocktail, cheese and fruit plates
and made sure everyone had a spiked eggnog

I'm spending Christmas in the basement with Louisa
reading poetry and pretending to sleep
I'm trying to block out all the noise from the people
walking around who aren't supposed to be in my house

It's been seven hours and counting and I finally hear
footsteps out the door, so I know
there are fewer people upstairs than there were
I'm really hoping the right ones are gone

Because I wouldn't be upset
if a couple of people were still here,
but I wouldn't be happy if some of the other ones were:
those who've invaded my home and disrupted my life

I'd hoped that if I avoided certain people as much as possible
I could still do holidays once a year, but I can't

Instead, I'm spending Christmas in the basement
reading poetry, curled up with the cat
wishing I could drink peppermint tea
by the living room fireplace with my mom
and say I'm sorry for ruining her Christmas

I'm not ready for these Christmases, these new times
I can't fake feeling joyful anymore
I wish I did have more to share,
especially with my mom,
but I've used up my smile
reporting and anchoring the news on TV

Today, I just couldn't fake it
Christmas in the basement was all I could do

I don't know what my mother told anyone:
Perhaps, that I was sick
Perhaps it's true, that I am

MOTHER TONGUE, or, **MY FAMILY SPEAKS ANOTHER LANGUAGE**

I tell my mother that I've outgrown my family
the same way Nona's children outgrew their pants

Nona would sew two inches of material
onto the bottom of her children's pant legs
even if it was orange corduroy and the pants, denim,
so they'd have pants with enough material
to cover their ankles and keep them warm

Being immigrant Italians,
Nona never added elastic to the waistband
Her children grew taller, but not fatter
Mostly, they worked hard
and when they weren't working, played kick the can

As my grandfather would tell the story:
In my family, we always had enough to eat
If we reached for seconds at the dinner table
Nono would slap our hand away and say
"You've had enough!"

I tell my mother, when she asks if I'll ever attend
holidays again with my Italian relatives
the way I used to enjoy growing up, I say
Yes, of course, as long as it's just our family
Then I wouldn't feel in any danger
the way I feel when those I don't trust
show up as well

I tell my mother that even if I did go, it's not like
I could have a real conversation with people
(even though we're all English speakers
who never learned Italian because Nona and Nono
wanted their children to be American)
I tell her, to me, when my family does speak to me,
the words come out in a language I don't understand:
it's as if they're speaking Greek and I speak Chinese

I tell my mother
it's not that I don't want to talk with my family
or hear what they might have to say
It's that when they ask me
How are you doing?
and *What have you been up to?*
and I respond with truthful answers:

I've been very sad
I cry every day
I keep looking for a job
No, I'm not dating anyone
Yes, I'm still writing
I'm having problems with my first book
Yes, tennis is OK but I hurt my back
and haven't been able to play for a few months

...and even now that things have improved:
Yes, I love my new talk show, it's so fun
I'm so grateful to have a job

I receive an awkward response*:*
Oh, so now you're a pundit!
You should be so proud of yourself
Not: *Fantastic!*
I'm so proud of you

This, from a family member
who once held public office,
now unable to use the talk show
I sent him to discuss:
Unions and labor
U.S. drone policy
Childhood poverty in America
Foreign policy with Syria

This family member,
unable to use the one language
we actually could speak to one another
as a way of connecting
Instead, I receive an archaic Latin response
from deep within the lizard brain

Cleaning the litter box this morning,
I'm reminded of when I cleaned it last month:
Louisa was by the box, meowing
but when I went to investigate,
I couldn't find anything wrong

She cried more, I thought she was sick
I nearly took her to the vet
I had cleaned the box and given her food
Nothing made any sense

Later, she jumped on my bed
and began pawing the covers
She'd just peed. I cleaned up the mess
and prepped to take her to the vet

When I went back to the box I realized
I'd put the cover on, the wrong way
The opening was against the wall:
she'd been trying to tell me she couldn't get inside

Even animals have a language
to tell you what they need
Louisa found a way to communicate with me
and spoke it loud and clear

Her message came through
as loud and clear as those orange corduroy strips
must have looked on the bottom of Nona's children's jeans

Nona's kids knowing, no matter what she tried to do,
those pants would keep coming up short,
like the childhoods they'd begun to outgrow

BIOPSY

The first time my mother got breast cancer
she, herself a doctor, knew what could happen
if you decided to get a lumpectomy after the initial biopsy
and some of the tainted tissue remained in the body

My mother chose to have her whole breast off
She said she valued her own life over the vanity of her breast
Besides, she said, she needed to be there
for the people she cared for, including her patients and family

When cancer appeared in her other breast,
she didn't hesitate: she told them to take off that breast, too
She joked about not needing to look pretty for a man because
after all, she never dated anyone after she and my father divorced

She advised my grandmother
to have one mastectomy, then another
The same with my great-aunts and her sister:
they all had their breasts off

I've tried to use a scalpel
to dissect the parts of my family I can handle,
surgically slicing and choosing holidays
I could emotionally survive

It wasn't always this way. When Grampa was alive
people honored him and got together no matter what
Those were the times I enjoyed the most:
as a little girl, with twenty relatives
crammed into our small apartment for birthdays

Things became tricky when my mother allowed
my father's children to live with us in our new house
She didn't want me to be alone and somehow thought
bringing my siblings in would be a good idea

At ten, I had no words to say
No, mom, please don't do it
Just you and me is OK
Instead, I began acting out more:
prank-calling my teacher, stealing from her desk
cheating on tests and mainly, being mean to my mother

When I moved in with my ex-fiancé in Binghamton
ten years ago, I discarded those people, my relatives
I created a new life with my ex's family:
one that was similar to mine, though wealthier
They too had young children and birthday parties
The got together for holidays and funerals
and even celebrated lesser occasions
like getting a new puppy

I embraced my new family:
I made chocolate cakes from scratch
Cornish hens for Christmas
and the Armenian cheese pastry, *boereg,* for funerals

When two days before our wedding
my ex decided not to marry me, I was
thrust back into the whirlwind of my own relatives:
people who didn't really know me,
people I no longer wanted to know

Because each time I tried to speak to them
they said the matter was private
More often, they said I was just a kid
(even in my thirties) and what did I know

In two weeks, my last great-aunt will be memorialized
Although I very much want to go, I won't attend
Those invited – and with whom I share blood –
have proven to me, they're really not my people
That despite our shared blood,
we're really not from the same tribe

Today, I surgically reconstruct
a new circle of friends in a new city and state
Like my mother after her breast cancer surgeries
this tainted tissue, I choose to let go

NINE: Transitions

WHERE DO I GO FROM HERE

My poetry teacher tells me not to get an MFA
because doing so would ruin me and my writing

My colleagues say I don't need a Masters in Journalism
noting the new host of The Today Show has a law degree

My mother says I'd always have a job if I became a nurse
and with a special certificate, I could even prescribe meds

My friend tells me interest rates are so low right now
I should get a bank loan and start my own business

My other friend says I should work in Public Relations
because my broadcast experience would be an asset
to promoting products on TV, the radio, and online

They say careers these days last up to fifteen years
I've had all training I need:
loss is one of life's greatest teachers

Thought I've tried, I have yet to discover
how to create a paycheck out of knowing myself well:
how to use what I didn't know I needed to learn, but did
and then spin it into gold

OPRAH WINFREY IS SCHEDULED TO SPEAK AT THIS YEAR'S HARVARD COMMENCEMENT

Oprah Winfrey is scheduled to speak
at this year's Harvard commencement
If there was ever anyone I wanted to be, it's Oprah
I would take her all in, even with any weight issues
and minus her billions of dollars

Oprah ended her popular talk show two years ago
after doing it for twenty-five years
I was fourteen when it began and before that,
we only had Phil Donohue to watch

With his salt and pepper hair Phil seemed sensitive,
but Oprah was different: with Patti LaBelle 80's hair,
she peeled back people's layers and got right to their guts
She shared her own stories of being sexually abused
by someone in her family, of growing up poor in the south,
of her youthful promiscuity

This year, I'll celebrate my twentieth college reunion
Even though I received my diploma in 1994, I entered
in 1989 and you get to keep your original class year
I've asked to be a 1993 class marshal
on Commencement day, because that will ensure
I'll get a proper seat to hear Oprah speak

I want to give her a copy of my first book,
tell her I've tried to be like her all along:
that I'm a TV news anchor and reporter like she was
and I want my own talk show, like hers

I want to read her my poems about my father and mother,
the ones about the unexpected breakup with my ex
I want to ask her to give me a chance
at hosting my own talk show on her new channel,
the Oprah Winfrey Network (OWN)

I don't know how close I'll ever get to Oprah Winfrey
I met her best friend, Gayle King,
at a journalism fundraiser in New York last month

I do know Oprah is the only big celebrity I care to meet
She doesn't need to give me keys to a free new car
I just want to be her new color purple

CLIMAX

The vast majority of women do not achieve orgasm
simply by having vaginal intercourse

If, however, women frequently requested additional stimulation
and those requests became the stipulation
for what constitutes satisfying sex for a woman
(in the same way orgasms in men are obvious,
because how can you not notice when a man has one)
then perhaps women today would become more accustomed
to asking for what they want and deserve,
in and out of the bedroom,
and would earn more than seventy-seven cents on a man's dollar

I read the 2012 article on the USC researchers who queried
hundreds of college students about marriage proposals
Most women said they still felt they needed a man to propose
while most men said it would be strange if a woman did

Specifically, the question was asked
if a woman *definitely* wanted the man to propose,
which warranted the vast majority of *yes's*
When that very same question was posed
inversely to men,
none at all checked the box

My cousin, who went to Yale, Oxford, and Princeton tells me,
after leaving Wall Street to birth five children,
she'd like to do something fulfilling outside the home
She said recently, her four-year-old daughter asked
What's that? when shown a picture of a woman
and next to it, a woman's suit and a briefcase
To which my friend replied,
It's a suit—and here is her briefcase
To which the little girl responded:
Mommy, girls don't work
Wringing her hands, confessing resentment, my cousin says
she has a hard time getting what she needs:
that she's always last in line

It's been said, there is no female Viagra
except the sound of a man running the vacuum cleaner

Still, if women began asking for more of what they needed
and if today's independent women
were more comfortable receiving, instead of always doing
we might be surprised at what kinds of barriers we'd break:

Sight
Sound
Glass ceilings

TEN: Afterlife

NAMING

-for the shooting victims in Newtown, Connecticut
December 15, 2012

Even her name sounds like a whisper—Emilie
Her father says she loved to draw:
That she carried markers and pencils
and would surprise-gift you with her sketches
In her picture, she looks like a child model:
the kind you find in stock footage
of the life you're supposed to try to attain,
the one with the white picket fence
the Golden Retriever, the younger brother
and the mother and father (who'd not yet divorced)

Her face was the first and the one that will linger—but seeing

Noah Ponzer, six: sturdy and handsome, even for his age
with a bush of dark hair, thick eyebrows
and head cocked to the side, just so,
sporting his corduroy jacket with the wide shearling collar
Would he be at home in a barn, a cowboy?
Or throwing long passes, the football quarterback?
Commanding orders, a construction foreman?
Already, a little man

Grace McDonnell, seven: proud of her pink hair bow
perfectly placed above her temple. Her round face
her smile—with lips unparted
A look of trust and vulnerability
softly piercing through her blue eyes

Catherine Hubbard, six: her fiery red bangs
touching her eyebrows, her innocent grin
Freckles on the apples of her cheeks
Orange, the color of the trees in autumn behind her
I imagine her in her ancestral land
of Leicestershire, England, where further
examination of her surname tells us
what we already knew: "Hug-bright"

Jessica Rekos, six: her eyes tinged with longing
the way a puppy's might be. I imagine her
playing American girl dolls with her friends
and later, with dark blue and gold pom-poms
cheering on Newtown's teams

Charlotte Bacon, six: white snow and bare trees
behind her, a missing front tooth. I see a free spirit:
a bundled-up artist-in-the-making
with polka dot hat and curly hair
Would she have chosen water-colored brush strokes?
Inks or crayons to write her words?
Silk fabric for designing long dresses?
Blue hydrangeas to create garden landscapes?

Olivia Engel, six: so tiny
Might she have been a ballet dancer?
She looks even younger than the other children
The blouse draping over her small shoulders
bears ruffles; a velvet headband adorns her hair
Perhaps she'd be nervous on stage, but still so pleased
when she'd finished and her parents would say just
how proud they are of her, and how well she performed

James Mattioli, six: could he be the class clown?
Crouching behind a pumpkin, his dark brown eyes
look like he just might be about to get into something
I wonder if he could be, as was discovered by
Pietro Mattioli in Siena 500 years ago,
allergic to cats? And whether instead, there may be
a chocolate lab at the Mattioli home

Josephine Gay, seven: gap-toothed with glasses
A spunky leprechaun in her green St. Patrick's Day hat
Her pink shirt bears an embroidered pink heart
over her breastbone. Her curiosity brims
beneath her smile. She looks as though she
one day might be a teacher or librarian

Caroline Previdi, six: long eyelashes and chin-length hair
Her wide smile exposes growing baby teeth inside
Her light blue plastic barrette pulls back the locks
her mother smoothed each morning
Might she have had three children of her own?

Dylan Hockley, six: Eager, composed
Would he be the next class president?
In his picture, he leans forward
His clear blue eyes and bright red shirt
seem to say *Here I am*

And the women: Principal Dawn Hochsprung
Psychologist Mary Sherlach, Teacher Lauren Rosseau
Special Ed Teacher Anne Marie Murphy
Teacher Victoria Soto
We remember Rachel Davino, as well
as the mother of it all, Nancy Lanza

Without pictures, we remember:
Daniel Barden, seven
Ana Marquez-Green, six
Madeline Hsu , six
Chase Kowalski, seven
Jesse Lewis, six
Jack Pinto, six
Avielle Richman, six
Benjamin Wheeler, six
and Allison Wyatt, also six

Today we speak the names of those who were lost
We remember the innocents who were taken
and the maternal instincts that kicked in to protect them

I wish for these children, for these women
to be rooted together in a new tree;
their lives, not chopped down
by a man whose name I will not speak

No, we shall remember their faces instead
We shall always speak their names

DYING

I want to die as my grandfather did:
in the fall, in November's pre-winter cold,
when the ground is still earthy and not yet frozen over
but when it's time for somber slumber and rest

On the PBS special *Facing Death*, they excavate:
exposing roots and all of what has yet to grow
The narrator says the dead matter to the living:
that accompanying the dying makes living worthwhile

My grandfather passed away
November first on All Saints Day
My mother, who still works as a doctor, tells me
she's already paid for her own funeral

The documentary's funeral director says
cremation has increased in popularity, but unlike
earth burials, people don't find it easy to keep step
with the quickness of mourning a cremated loved one
Everyone in my family had always been buried
until cousin Frances was cremated in 2007,
and aunt Rachel in 2011

My mother tells me she already purchased the plot
where I, and perhaps other family members,
will be buried: in the same group of graves
where my aunt and grandparents now rest

After recent family disruptions, my mother tells me
she shall have a private funeral:
not the one she'd first envisioned, like the ones
my grandparents and great-aunts and uncles had
The ones with hundreds of guests and lunch at Carbone's
or a family member's home, afterwards

No, my mother tells me, as she always has,
preserving one's dignity in life, is what matters:
that what's needed most before our imminent passing
is to prepare ourselves

OBIT

To the public, she was perhaps best known as a poised news broadcaster, sitting on the desk or reporting breaking news on the streets of New York, Philadelphia, or Boston. But to her family, Frances Marguerite Maximé, known publicly as Francesca Maximé, was a family woman who enjoyed spending time cooking at home for holidays and baking cookies for friends and colleagues. Ms. Maximé was born to Haitian-Dominican father Asbel Benony Maximé (deceased) and Italian-American mother Dr. Janet Magnani of Ashland, Massachusetts, an emergency room physician from whom she learned the importance of charitable work.

Francesca became passionate about many causes over the years, most recently the animal adoption and animal rescue umbrella organization "Celebrity Catwalk," for which she hosted an event in June and was scheduled to host an event, in December. While living in Florida, she sat on the Board of the Pensacola Opera and the National Coalition against Addiction and Drug Dependence. She also hosted many fundraisers including ones for the Pensacola Ballet, the Santa Rosa Kids House and the Gulf Coast Kids House, aiding abused children. Perhaps her proudest achievement was successfully launching a curbside recycling program in Pensacola, which still exits to this day.

A Harvard graduate with a sharp wit and penchant for poetry, Francesca found her calling in journalism and interviewing, having talked with some of the country's most influential leaders and entertainers, from Robert Duvall, Matt Damon and Jessica Simpson, to Senators Charles Schumer, John Kerry, President George Bush, and Vice President Dan Quayle. She loved working on deadline and being the first to break news, but also loved the intricacies involved in telling a good story with pictures and sound.

Ms. Maximé often wrote poetry about her grandfather Louis P. Magnani, also deceased, and how the strength of his character was borne out not only in physical hard work as a mason, but also in word and deed. Francesca's close friends included those in Pensacola, FL and in Binghamton, NY where she also once resided and where she adopted her beloved cat, Louisa.

Ms. Maximé is survived by her mother, her half-sister and her two half-brothers. She also leaves behind uncles, aunts and cousins on both her father's and mother's side.

In lieu of flowers, it is asked that donations be made to "Rosie's Place," a shelter for homeless women in Boston. A wake will be held from five to nine on Thursday evening, the eighth of November at John A. Matarese funeral home in Ashland. A mass will be held at St. Cecelia's at nine o'clock Friday morning. Burial will take place at Wildwood Cemetery immediately following the mass.

BLACK AND WHITE
-In memory of Camilla Martin
February 4, 2013

They are white socks with black snowflakes
spaced about the ankle and ringed about the toes

They are ten percent angora, ten percent cashmere
The rest, acrylic fiber

They were Christmas gifts eight years ago
from my aunt-in-law's mother, Camilla
Along with an identical pair and their colored inverse,
the mainly black ones are now threadbare in spots
with holes worn through the heels,
the balls of my feet, and my right pinky toe

On the eve of this massive February snowstorm
coinciding with New England's Blizzard of '78,
I remember being buried in four feet of snow
at my grandparents' house and how my mother
miraculously drove home from work in the storm

I anticipate the heavy, delicate white flakes
coming down into this evening and overnight,
sure to pile up and create a dense and pure fortress ,
somehow turning everything old into something new

Tonight, the chill in my toes
is once again warmed
by these soft and short fuzzy socks

The ones I always select when a storm is coming
The ones I'll never again receive as a gift
The ones I can no longer buy

GONE

Zia Mary had a moustache, big hips, and white hair, but just like my mother used to have a white skunk streak, Zia Mary had a dark one above her left ear. Her face was thin for someone so sturdy in her lower half. She always looked at you in earnest and smiled, resembling my Aunt Rachel. Mary was a not-as-pretty version of:

Zia Isabelle's daughter now confesses she was a taskmaster. You wouldn't know it from her rose-hued cheeks, her soft skin like peaches, her bright eyes. She looked like her sister, but was rounder in appearance and in spirit. While Zia Mary made her home in Framingham, Zia Isabelle was on what was described as "the wrong side of the tracks," in Hopedale.

Zia Louisa's husband beat her, her sons ended up in jail. We never knew or heard much about her husband Oliver, but we knew he wasn't good to Zia. Louisa played organ and loved to sing. As big as she was (and she was very big, with a rounded pregnant-like tummy, big hips and a big bottom) she had the most delicate and amazing handwriting, as did all of Nona's girls. She pulled back her hair in a neat little bun. Her left incisor poked out when she smiled, which somehow, she seemed to do often. Her daughters Patti and Janice, although I now see them rarely, remind me more of her as time passes: persevering, just like their mother before them.

Zia Margaret was the most stout and looked more like my grandfather than her sisters. Shorter hair, not quite as pretty, she had one son—but raised her nieces, Kathleen and Mary, when her brother Frank's wife became ill. Margaret ensured they excelled in school, were polite and learned the piano. Margaret married Uncle Mando and they bought a house in downtown Ashland, where she and I played Rummy 500 and Crazy 8's after school. I'd ride my green Schwinn bike there from Grampa's house. She served me tea in bone china teacups. We made polenta and *cupalettis* (tortellini). We called them *un-veng*.

Uncle Joe we called Uncle Tootie, and he was a janitor at my middle school. He was sweet and smelled like wood and cologne, like the wood he loved to carve and shellac into hanging wall plaques and coffee tables. He had a moustache that tickled when he kissed you hello. He would soak Bing cherries in alcohol, and give them out at

Christmastime. He and Autie Lola, a devoted mom to Joe and Jeffrey and a smoker until her death of cancer, lived in a little house on Myrtle Street in Ashland their grandson now lives in.

Zia Diddie, Aunt Pauline, lived with Uncle Benny in Marlboro on Main Street. They had one daughter Linda, who had four children. Zia Diddie, the youngest, became a secretary and was the family record keeper. She organized everyone on index cards, and kept a shoe collection encased in glass in the dining room. Her husband was a cobbler, so it made sense.

Zia Eleanor lived in Bridgeport in an old apartment with her Spanish husband. Don Armando and had two children, Linda and Donald. Linda was born with poor eyesight and had to wear thick glasses. Her husband never forgave Zia for Linda's disability and while Zia took her daughter everywhere, Linda died at forty-three. Zia Eleanor worked as a telephone operator for thirty years. When I graduated from college, she gave me over three hundred dollars to buy wall art for my first apartment. She was my favorite great-aunt. We had a special connection. Today, fifteen years after her death, there's still no headstone to mark her grave.

Cousin Frances, my namesake, died of bile duct cancer. She'd married Ben the Jewish car salesman, and never had children although she loved them. A gorgeous woman with high-fashion sense, she was the first to go to college in the Magnani family. Her mother Angie, the eldest of the Zias, had married Uncle Pino. Angie, I knew the least. Her daughter Frances became one my "other mothers." She was always with me on the other end of the phone.

And who could forget my Grampa Louie. Entirely imperfect, he was a tool and die maker and father of five. A stone mason and gardener who loved to sing, play bocce and cribbage, shoot pool and watch bird in the backyard.

What I wouldn't give to have them all in my mother's house
singing Christmas carols this year
Eating *torte*, sipping coffee royals
the way we used to, when I was a child

ELEVEN: Living

GOOD OMEN

I think it's a magic sign, my mother says
when I tell her that sitting outside while reading,
a hummingbird came to me twice this afternoon
beating its wings so fervently the first time,
I didn't notice its green sheen

Yesterday I found out they selected me to anchor
the noon news program on a Turkish TV station
that resembles a CNN international or BBC America
This, after six months of not working in this economy
My unemployment is set to run out soon

It came, just in time:
this tiny bird, the size of my thumb,
flitting back and forth and then holding steady,
right before my eyes

My mother says
There must be something special about you
for it to come here and hover a foot away from my face

For it to visit me twice, without lingering
to display its delicate might

WE CAN TALK ABOUT THESE THINGS BECAUSE IT'S DIFFERENT NOW

When you were visiting me in Brooklyn this week, mother,
you came to bring my laundry that you'd done at home in Boston
Five large bags of it: big blue IKEA tote bags
all full of clean tennis outfits, jeans, towels, and underwear

There's only one place in my studio apartment to even put it all:
in front of my desk. It's the same spot where you usually place
your overnight bag. At eight A.M. Tuesday,
after three days of the laundry sitting there,
before I had my coffee, you asked me to put it away

It wasn't how I wanted to start my day
I made that clear, huffing around shoving t-shirts into drawers,
sweatpants into my armoire, nightgowns in their bins
Two days later while walking in Prospect Park and three days
into my first week of once again being unemployed, I tell you
maybe I can use the time I have to get more exercise like this:
to make salads and eat healthier and lose some weight

Two days later, standing in front of the kitchen sink, you tell me
at seventy-two, after working as a doctor for forty-five years, you
Need to have more fun in your life.
Just like you said, (that I'd said)
I needed to go on a diet

The words hung in the air like a Portuguese Man-of-War
on the ocean's surface: its invisible poison tentacles,
long and gangly, stinging deep below

But instead of becoming women of war
like we've often been, we just talked
You said it wasn't what you meant, that I'd brought it up
You apologized
I said I knew you weren't trying to hurt my feelings
and I resisted sulking, as I had when I put away the laundry

You're in therapy again and tell me
you want to have a "good relationship"
I say if we can survive a week together in my tiny studio apartment
with the only communication issue, a tat over laundry or weight,
then we're doing pretty good

It took another family betrayal to bring us together:
one that this time, didn't even come from your relatives

You've chosen to be with me, mother
You've come here, and we can talk easily

About the things we never spoke of before
About the things we still cannot say

THANKSGIVING PRAYER

What you gave me
(which I'm sure you didn't know you gave me)
was the greatest gift:
Wholeness, peace of mind:
an ending to trying to put together
the puzzle of my life

When people would say to me
You have to be grateful for what you have
and I still didn't feel grateful for everything
(even though I knew I should be grateful for everything)
I tried to understand why I didn't feel that way
Now I know

When people would say
You just have to not eat the cupcake or pizza or pretzels
and I knew that all I had to do
was say no to the food and I wouldn't be fat
that I understood, cognitively, what they were saying
But I still couldn't explain why I'd then eat it anyway

When people would say
You just have to exercise more: you'll get fit and lose weight
and I knew what they were saying was true
but I couldn't figure out why I didn't want to exercise,
even if I was healthy enough to do so, and why I'd prefer to
remain at a heavier weight and not move my body
Now, I know the answers

After years of therapy
and years of digging down deep into my past
my relationships with my father, my mother
my family including half-siblings, aunts and uncles
everything exploded when my ex
whom I'd been with for seven years
told me he didn't want to get married
just two days before our wedding
After that, I was forced to look hard
at my life in a way I'd never anticipated
and I began finding some answers

One, that inappropriate contact with my father
was a form of sexual abuse. I learned it had
dictated my longing for love and relationships
from men who were unworthy

I learned much of my frustration towards my mother
was over her allowing me to see my father
when she knew he wasn't healthy

I learned I was frustrated with my mother
for bringing so many people into my life
like her former step-children, who came to live with us,
when I was accustomed to being raised as an only child

With that incest resources counselor in Boston I began to investigate
why I had such self-loathing:
why I thought I was a bad person inside
and why I then ended up doing things that were bad
to me, for me, or to others

like eating too much food, driving too fast
drinking too much, and spending too much on credit cards
Or sniping at my mother,
having problems with authority at work
and sniping at my ex-fiancé

I learned that because I always wanted my father's love
(and he was incapable of giving it to me or anyone)
that as little children, we take on the thought
this phenomenon is "our fault"
and if we're better people, we'll be able
to get parents who cannot, to love us

It was a fallacy, of course
In my own way, I tried until the day he died:
I longed for my father's love
The wish that he would love me,
once a deep wound, today is healed

When I left my first counselor
and found a new therapist in New York City
I asked her two things:
*Why don't I believe the good things
about myself that people tell me?*
and *Why don't I feel like I deserve
good things?*

Again, these negative thoughts
were brought on by the young girl inside me,
who thought all the bad that had happened
with her father, was her fault to fix:
that it was her responsibility to make things right
She would do anything for his affection

It was an incorrect assumption,
but one I carried for over thirty-five years:
one that brought me into an unhealthy relationship
with a man also incapable of unconditional love

I say these things because now, everything's clarified
My relationship with my mother is whole:
your actions have brought past issues to a head
I no longer have any questions, I am free
This gift, this Thanksgiving, is truly one to celebrate

I no longer feel bad and have to do things for others out of lack
I can choose to act out of wholeness and abundance,
not just because I feel so abandoned and unloved
that I have a false compassion for people in need,
or for those in worse circumstances than mine

I no longer need someone love me:
I love and accept myself
I know in my heart I'm a good person
Now I can choose to do good and healthy things
for myself and for others, because I want to,
and because it's the right thing to do
I can do them without hurting or abandoning myself:
I can give bountifully, without sacrifice

I am whole, the hole has been filled
The pieces are all in place
The maze deciphered, I'm now free
I release all old questions
I no longer need to investigate

It will be easy not to judge,
to be compassionate,
and genuinely grateful

I will no longer grin and bear it:
there will be no need
to steel myself through situations

I choose healthy environments:
those which are life-enhancing
for myself and those I care for

If people cannot see, hear or feel
the love with which I act,
I need not do for those people

I will no longer seek reward,
satisfaction and approval from others
I am satisfied with myself

My reward is my sanity
and my right relationship with my mother
whose love knows no bounds

These are my gifts this year
This Thanksgiving, this Christmas

They're all I ever needed
They're all I'll ever need

About the Author

Francesca Marguerite Maximé is a poet and television news anchor and reporter in New York City. Francesca was born in Chicago to an Italian-American mother and a Haitian-Dominican father and grew up outside of Boston. She graduated from Harvard with a degree in English Literature. After college, she studied poetry at SUNY Binghamton under Maria Mazziotti Gillan. When she moved to New York City in 2009, she also began working with poet Laura Boss.

Outside of her work as a broadcast journalist and poet, Maxime spends time competing on several USTA tennis teams. She also frequently hosts events for animal rescue causes, is a firm believer in recycling, and enjoys baking and cooking.

Her first book, *Rooted: a verse memoir* was published by NYQ Books in 2012. Maximé is also being nominated for a Pushcart Prize in poetry.

Made in the USA
Charleston, SC
21 April 2013